Dedicated to Mom and Dad

Who gave me the courage to try, the love to care, and the desire to succeed

and

to my loving husband, Charlie

Acknowledgments

I would first like to thank two very special people in my life who have provided me with the facts of our ancestors dating back to the middle of the Eighteenth century. They are my Aunt Florence and Cousin Rose. Without their memories of the past, I would not have been able to find out so much about my grandparents and their grandparents. They provided a treasure of memories for all our relatives to share. Their memories are the lifeline to our past.

To my Cousin Bill Thomas—a very special thank you for sharing the information that he accumulated from archives which traced the Ellien, Jasman, and Yassomedes families as far back as the 1750s. His compassion and zeal to find out about our ancestors and then share it with his relatives are most appreciated.

I am most grateful to the Cury and Dawahare families; Frank and Jennie Abdoo's family and, in particular, their children Lloyd and Martha and grandchild, Jennie Ann, for caring about their roots; and my cousin, Tom Cury, for supporting my search for the history of the Cury family in Kentucky. Martha gave me the idea to gather the family anecdotes from our relatives so that one day our children's children could read about our shared past. Her untimely death prevented Martha from writing her story. However, her memories are my memories and are published in this book. Other cousins who have contributed to my research are Dick and Buddy, as well as Bob, Mary Joan, and Marian.

My brother, Bill, has played a major role in helping me to recall many wonderful, as well as sad, memories that we will always cherish. To my lovely daughter, Cathy, and two wonderful sons, Charles and Stephen, I say thank you for being there to support me in this endeavor to record the history of the Ellien and Cury family. Without their encouragement, I would not have been able to be steadfast in my search for the truth about our families.

Four very special educators to whom I will forever be grateful for laying the foundation in my educational career are Dr. Frank Smith, Jr.; Herbert Balish; Isaac Feinberg; and Miriam Zucker. Without their support and guidance, I don't think I would have gone as far as I did in the field of education.

Words will never express my gratitude to my husband, Charlie, who has always been near my side to lend an ear, provide information when I needed it, and—most of all—to assure me that I would complete my memoirs.

A very special thank you to Carl Makower, and Michael D'Ambrosio, two of my colleagues and personal friends, whose friendship at Fort Hamilton High School will forever remain in my heart. I must thank my friend, Connie Von Frolio, who was extremely supportive and helpful in proof reading my material for the book and keeping me focused on my work.

I am forever grateful to my high school friend, Elsa Anderson Van Bergen. As the editor of my memoirs, she helped me to complete my work. She was honest and sincere in her suggestions and helped me to focus on every detail. She is one of those friends that my Dad said I could count on one hand.

Although Mom and Dad are not here to read these memoirs of the past and the present, they instilled in my brothers, George (who, sadly, passed away at the age of 58 in February 1995) and, Bill, as well as in me, the passion to know what we want, the drive to achieve success, and the tenacity to never forget our roots. Our parents always encouraged us to be proud of these roots which stem from as far away as Greece, Lebanon, and Syria. They established a sound foundation of family values that culminated in a social and work ethic involving our Church, our family, and our Christian beliefs of what it means to live in a free and democratic nation where respect for our fellow human beings, our country, and ourselves take priority.

Table of Contents

(Opposite page) This portrait of me was commissioned during my tenure as principal of Fort Hamilton High School in Bay Ridge, Brooklyn, 1989-99, and now hangs permanently in the school library. The artist, Mary Bucher, did such a wonderful job that the picture became one of my personal favorites. My painting joined a long procession of others honoring past principals, but it had the distinction of being the first picture of a woman as principal of Fort Hamilton since the opening of the high school in September 1941.

(Opposite page) Portrait of Alice Cury Farkouh by Mary Bucher, 1999, courtesy of Portraits Inc.

My dream was to one day return to my high school as a teacher. I never dreamt that I would return as the principal of the school. Look into the eyes of the dreamer and know that you should

Never Say You Can't...Never Say You Can't...

Chapter I

In the Beginning

One by one my great-grandparents came to America from Lebanon and Syria at the turn of the twentieth century. They fled from the Ottoman Turks by seeking refuge in America. *No!* They were not going to be forced to have their young men serve in the military for a country that ravaged their land and raped their wives and daughters. My great-grandparents wanted to settle in America—the land of the free and the home of the brave. To understand why they had this dream to come to America, you would have to understand their way of life going back to the late eighteenth century.

In the 1770s, George Yassomedes, great-great-grandfather on my mother's side, was born in Cyprus, a Greek Island in the Mediterranean Sea south of Turkey under Ottoman rule. George was one of seven brothers and lived to be 110 years old. He married a Syrian woman and had a son, Gregory. Gregory (1786—1892) married a Syrian woman and had a son, Louzy. Louzy (1836—1908) married a Syrian woman and had two sons, Elias and Alexander (1859—1928). There is little known about Elias' family. However, Alexander's family moved to Alexandreta, now a city in Turkey. Since 1516, it had been a province in Syria that was under Turkish rule. In 1890, it was still Syria. By 1900, it was in Turkey and part of the Ottoman Empire. In 1907, it was part of

My mother's grandfather, Alexander Yassomedes, as a young boy (standing left); my great-grand father, Louzy Yassomedes (seated); and my great-uncle, Elias Yassomedes, also as a young boy (standing right). *(c. 1860)*

Syria under French rule. It was not until 1939 that Turkey annexed Alexandreta.

In Alexandreta, Alexander was a millionaire. He owned property and was a well-known money lender. He met a beautiful young girl named Mary Ruttle. Mary's father was a rich merchant marine who owned several ships. The family was from Tripoli, Syria. Today, Tripoli is part of Lebanon. However, Lebanon was still part of Syria when Alexander and Mary met.

It is important to realize that the people living on the mountains of Lebanon considered themselves Lebanese at that time. The Bible (Psalms 104:16) mentions the Cedars of Lebanon, "The trees of the Lord are full of sap; The Cedars of Lebanon which he planted." In fact, the Cedars of Lebanon are mentioned many times in the Old Testament. In the New Testament, Jesus is said to have walked through the area, carrying the Word of God, and actually healing many. The Cedars of Lebanon were used to make shields, various wooden implements and majestic temples. In the Book of Judges the five Philistine cities, the Canaanites, the Sidonians, and the Hivites lived in the mountains of Lebanon. It is said in the Book of Kings I that King Solomon spoke "of trees and plants from the Lebanon cedars . . . " In fact, the Cedars of Lebanon were important in developing the coast for 4,800 years. As early as 5000 B.C., the Phoenicians— or Canaanites, as they were called—settled in Beirut, Tyre, Sidon, Bybos, and even had a colony in Carthage in 900 B.C. They were conquered later by many: the Babylonians, Persians, Macedonians, Romans, Byzantines, Arab caliphs, Crusaders, Egyptians, Ottoman Turks, and the French in 1918.

Finally in 1941, but suspended until 1943, Lebanon was granted its independence from the French. However, the French stayed until the end of 1946. From 1861 through 1941, local provinces exercised some authority under the rule of the Ottomans. And through all of this, the Phoenicians remained.

My maternal side of the family (Yassomedes) decided to leave Syria. In 1910, the Jasman family (the family's original Greek name appeared as Yassimidis on the manifest of the ship which brought them to the United States but that name was changed to Jasman by American immigration officials when the family arrived at Ellis Island in New York) decided to immigrate to America from Alexandreta because of fear of the Turks. The Turks had slaughtered over three million Armenians and were feared by everyone under their rule. My great-grandfather, Alexander, saw rowboats taking hundreds of people to ships at the port of Al Mina near Tripoli. He asked his brother, Elias, what was happening and was told that the Turks were coming. Fearing for the safety of his five girls and four sons, he decided to make plans to go to America with his children and his wife, Mary Ruttle (my great-grandmother). His five daughters were: Tzemila (Jenny),

My mother's family, the Elliens: (Front row seated L to R) Giddi George and Sitti Nellie. (Back row standing L to R) Aunt Florence; Aunt Virginia; Uncle Alex; my mother—Katherine; and Aunt Emily. *(c. 1930)*

Nazly (my maternal grandmother and known to me as Sitti Nellie), Anastasia (Aunt Annie), Katy, and Athena. The four sons were: George, Ebrahim, and twins Nagy and Kamel. His sons had already been forced to register in the Turkish army as required but had not entered the service. Alexander had to work feverishly and in secret. He had to get his family out of Tripoli, a town settled by many Greeks in Syria. Now, it is in Lebanon. He sold and gave away his property and business to his brother and close friends. He was able to raise an additional $50,000 for passage money for his family. Mary packed what she could and, within a few days, they were gone. Alexander placed his cash in a money bag and belted it around his waist. He was indeed a wealthy merchant but was giving up a great deal of wealth to seek a different life for his precious family. This plan was his lifeline to America.

My grandmother, Sitti Nellie, (seated left) along with her sisters, Katy (standing center), and Jenny (seated right), with their mother, Mary (seated center). *(c. 1920).*

My great-aunt, Athena Jasman (Yassomedes), (standing left) with my great-grandmother, Mary (standing right). *(c. 1940)*

Alexander boarded the ship, the *SS Patris*, from the port of Piraeus in Greece on February 28, 1910. They arrived in New York City on Palm Sunday, March 18, 1910. The ship's manifest listed the family as "Alexandros Yassimidis." When the *SS Patris* arrived in New York harbor, immigration officials interpreted the name Yassomedes as Jasman in spite of the fact that the manifest listed their name as Yassomedeas. Later on, other family members changed their new family name of Jasman to Jasmin. Imagine how immigration officials made decisions that affected the heritage of its arrivals for generations to come — starting with their family name.

Alexander and Mary were finally in America. Their children ranged in age from 7 to 29. Their fifth daughter, Katy, was not allowed to come to stay in America because of an eye infection. Nine years later, Katy and her husband, Philip Sahady, immigrated to America. They had treated Katy's eyes in Italy on the

Sitti Nellie in America *(c. 1910)*.

way and were very lucky to get Katy into the country. Sitti Nellie, (Sitti is the Arabic word for "my grandmother") was elated to have her sister, Katy, finally arrive in America.

Sitti Nellie was 23 when she arrived in America and 24 when she married her husband, George, on September 23, 1911. Giddi George (Giddi is the Arabic word for "my grandfather") was an emigrant from Homs, Syria. Although Sitti Nellie was 24, she always told her children that she got married at the age of 19. Well, things haven't changed today. Our ancestors didn't tell the truth about their ages in those days and many of us still don't. My mother and her sisters told the truth about their age. Perhaps that was because they were first generation. Forget about my father's side. Dad, his brother, Tom, and his sister Jennie were the only honest ones when it came to being truthful about their ages. Human nature? No, just vanity.

My paternal grandfather, Giddi Bady Cury (the first name later changed to Beddy) was born in 1877, and my paternal grandmother (Sitti Deeba) was born in 1875. They came from a small village called Ruchum in Horan, Syria. Ruchum is south of Damascus and is now located in the Golan Heights. Giddi Cury and his beautiful bride came from prominent families. Giddi Cury's father was a "sheik" in his village. That's a word in Arabic which has special meaning. Traditionally, it was used to describe a village leader but it was also, and still is, used to describe a man who is held in special esteem within his village, social group, or family. The Cury family was Christian and very religious. Legend goes that when St. Peter, St. Paul, and St. Thomas traveled along the roads radiating from Damascus, they arrived in Ruchum and converted many of the Jewish families, one of which was Dad's ancestors. Dad's original family name was Alkhoury which, when translated from Arabic, meant "the priest." My father didn't tell us when Alkhoury was changed to Cury, but it was probably at the turn of the twentieth century.

Giddi Cury married Sitti Deeba Salik in the early 1890s and they had three daughters: Thana, Hannah, and Mary; and one son, Galeb. Giddi Cury was known for "having a bad temper" and carrying a gun. Around the beginning of the twentieth century, he shot and killed two local Bedouin tribesmen on two different occasions. His father decided to send him immediately to America. Giddi Cury quickly packed, taking with him a large sum of money, and left for America without his wife and four children. In America, Giddi Cury could not speak a word of English. So, he bought himself a pocket Arabic-English dictionary and carried it in his shirt pocket for many years. I don't remember seeing it, but Giddi wanted to learn how to speak the language of this country. In fact, all my relatives on both sides wanted to become part of America's customs and traditions. Citizenship in the United States was their number one priority. For every word someone said in English, Giddi would pull out the dictionary and have them point to the English word. He would then memorize it

My father's family, the Curys: (Front row seated L to R) Aunt Mary; my father—William Beddy (just a small boy in this picture); and Uncle Tom. (Middle row seated L to R) K. Cury; my grandmother—Sitti Deeba, and my grandfather—Giddi Beddy. (Back row standing L to R) Giddi Beddy's sister, Selma; Uncle Galeb and his bride, Anastasia (Annie); and Aunt Thana. *(c. 1911)*

using the Arabic counterpart. That is how he learned our language in America.

Giddi Cury soon bought a factory in New York and produced silk shirts and blouses for both men and women. His business thrived so much that he extended it to additional silk garments for women, a very productive commodity at the turn of the twentieth century. In addition to doing well in the factory, Giddi Cury invested his money in real estate in the Bronx and he soon became a wealthy landlord. He returned many years later to Horan, Syria. He found his young wife waiting anxiously for his return. She had taken care of the children. Her father-in-law had taken care of her and the children. She lived like royalty in Syria while she was away from Giddi Cury. Giddi Cury brought Sitti Deeba, and his four children (Galeb, Thana, Hannah, and Mary) back to America. At the immigration center in New York City, officials noticed Hannah's eye infection and deported her back to Syria. This was a sad day for the Cury family. They were never to see Hannah return to America, but the family always kept in touch with Aunt Hannah and her family as the decades passed.

The Curys settled in lower Manhattan at 189 Broome Street for a while and then moved to 481 Third Street in Brooklyn. During this period of time, Giddi Cury brought many of his relatives to America. His brother, Dahan Cury, (later called D. Cury) immigrated to America and stayed with Giddi Cury for awhile. However, D. Cury wanted to pursue a career in retailing like his brother. So he decided to travel down south and settle in Norton, Virginia. Giddi had his sister, Selma, come to America and stay with him. During her stay with Giddi, she met a man called Serur Frank Dawahare. Serur was born in a village near Damascus, Syria, not too far from Horan. He, like many other immigrants, had fled Syria to escape religious persecution. Serur, like Giddi Cury, spoke no English when he arrived here. However, he soon learned how to speak English because he wanted to assimilate into American society as Giddi Cury did. The English dictionary became his guide like Giddi's. Unlike Giddi, Serur had very little money. However, he was a very learned man who always spoke eloquently at special occasions. He was called "the speech-maker" of the family.

After taking a job at a sweat shop in New York City, Serur met Giddi's sister, Selma, at a party in Giddi's house, first seeing her as she was washing dishes. It must have been "love at first sight." Within a few months, they were married. D. Cury told Serur about the coal mines in Kentucky and Virginia and the opportunity to make a better living for Selma. He left Selma with Giddi and went "pack peddling" merchandise in Virginia and Kentucky. After saving some money, he sent for Selma and they moved to East Jenkins, Kentucky. As time passed, Selma and

Serur had eleven children (eight boys and three girls). Serur did so well that he opened up a small store and sold merchandise to pack peddlers. More time passed and he opened up a bigger store in 1922 in Neon, Kentucky. Unfortunately, Selma died in 1939 at the age of 49. Serur and his family continued to work hard and this eventually resulted in a dynasty of department stores. Like Giddi Cury, Serur taught himself to read and write the English language. He kept his own books and even prepared his own taxes. The Dawahare family had a very strong work ethic. They knew the value of sweat and toil. There is a story passed down from generation to generation in the Dawahare family based on an old Arabic story told in all the villages of the Arab world. It is often referred to as "The Stick Story." Evidently, Serur had given each of his eight sons a stick and asked each one to break the stick. Then he put all the pieces together and had each one try to break the bundle of sticks. No one could. The moral of his story was "If you stick together, you will never be broken." That is what they learned at home with their father as a role model. Giddi Cury, and his sons and grandchildren, stayed close to the Dawahare family for many decades. It is amazing that, even today, the Cury family and the Dawahare family, including many of Selma and Serur's children, still communicate with each other and try to keep the past in the present. That is probably what Serur meant in his "Stick Story."

My Uncle Tom was born in 1907, followed by my father in 1909, and my Aunt Jennie in 1912. In 1913, Sitti Deeba was pregnant with her last child, Rose. She took her sons, Tom and my Dad, and her daughter Jennie to Syria. It was Sitti Deeba's dream that Rose would be born in her homeland. The other children— Galeb, Thana, and Mary—were left to work in Giddi's factory. Soon after her arrival in Horan, Syria, Sitti Deeba gave birth to Rose. And then World War I broke out, in August 1914, and no one was allowed to return to America until after the war ended. Giddi Cury sent money to his family while he continued to stay in America with his son and daughter-in-law, Galeb and Annie, and his daughters, Mary and Thana. Annie was Sitti Nellie's sister. Aunt Jennie would tell her children for many decades how they "were stuck in Syria during World War I." She would tell her grandchild, Jennie Ann, about how food was so scarce in the Middle East that they had to scrape the ground for main staples. My father kept this experience to himself and never shared with us the hardships his family endured during their stay in Syria at that time. Obviously, the children born in America wanted to come home, and come home as soon as possible. At the end of the war in 1917, Sitti Deeba returned with her children and reunited with Giddi Cury.

My father got the title of Sheik William, like his father. None of the other sons were called "sheiks," just Dad. Perhaps, it was because Dad was very handsome and had blue eyes as Giddi Cury did (blue eyes were not too common in our family). My future husband's family, Shukri and Marie Farkouh, came from Homs Syria, a location not far away from Giddi Cury's village in Horan. Blue eyes were quite common in their families. All of my husband's uncles on his mother's side had blue eyes as well. I remember asking my father where he got the blue eyes. After all, his family came from Syria where the population usually had olive skin and dark eyes. He reminded me that when the Crusaders came down from the North and entered the Middle East during Medieval times, they ravished and raped the women. The fair skin, light blue and green eyes, and blonde hair became recessive genes of the people from the Mediterranean area. Interesting....

Dad's handsome face and stunning icy blue eyes set him apart from others. He had the intelligence and eloquence of his father. Dad was fluent in English, Arabic, and French and knew how to read, write, and sing in Arabic as well. He was also a superb dancer. He could dance all the ballroom dances, including the popular tango. Dad even styled his hair to look like Rudolph Valentino in the early days when Valentino was one of the most popular screen stars in the movie theatres. Whenever Dad was at a Hafli or a dinner dance or wedding, he would lead the Arabic

"Dabkee." The Dabkee was a traditional dance where men and women formed a chain and danced in unison with a male dancer leading the way and waiving a handkerchief in the air. The musician played on a clay drum while the dancers stamped their feet using a variety of steps. I often look at my own wedding tapes and see Dad, handkerchief in one hand, leading the Dabkee with me next to him in my wedding dress. He led the dance line with the gusto of a leader. Yes, he was "our Sheik." I didn't find out until later on in life that Giddi Cury had a beautiful voice like Dad. In America, Giddi Cury was a cantor at St. Nicholas Cathedral in Brooklyn, New York. It was known originally as a "Syrian Orthodox Church." It was not until the 1980's that the official name became "Antiochian Orthodox Church."

Giddi Cury must have been fascinated with the popular music of the time. When his daughter, Mary, got married to Saba Ajalat in 1926, in Giddi and Sitti Deeba's home on Third Street, he played music from the famous Italian opera tenor, Enrico Caruso, at the wedding ceremony and reception. Caruso had died five years before, but his music and songs were still played in every household, regardless of nationality.

Giddi Cury, Dad, and Rose G. all had beautiful voices, but no one in the family was as talented musically as Aunt Mary and Uncle Saba's younger son, Buddy. In 1943, Buddy sang on the Major Bowes Amateur Hour. It was one of the country's best-known radio talent shows at the time. He was also a member of the Army Symphonic Orchestra and sang, from 1953 to 1956, in the Army's Voice of America.

Tragedies ran in the family as well. Sitti Deeba had a very serious accident in 1936 in her home on 481 Third Street. The story goes that after cleaning her daughter Rose's vest with Naptha lighter fluid, she dumped the liquid into the toilet bowl. The gas hot water boiler was located right next to the toilet. It was soon to be bathing time and the family needed hot water. She decided to light the boiler. Tragically, when she threw the wooden match into the bowl, the Naptha fluid burst into flames and all of Sitti

Sitti Deeba in America

Deeba's clothes immediately caught fire. Screaming and hysterical, Sitti Deeba ran outside for help. The cold air fed the ferocious fire on her body. A passerby took his coat off and smothered the flames. Sitti Deeba was rushed to Belleview Hospital where she sustained third degree burns all over her body. When she was released from the hospital, Uncle Galeb took her home to his house where she died later of infections from the burns.

Before this horrible tragedy, Sitti Deeba had been absolutely beautiful. My mother showed us a large oval portrait of my grandmother where she was dressed in a Victorian blouse with long sleeves. Her long hair was gracefully pulled away from her face giving her the appearance of a stately queen. Her portrait does not show any visible markings on her face, but photography can be deceiving. Mom would tell us how Giddi Cury's bride in the old country was covered with tattoos all over her body. The premise was that "no other man would look at her beauty but her husband." Actually, this was a custom in Syria and Lebanon when brides were married into well-to-do families. Henna was used to create the tattoos. If Sitti Deeba did not have the picture taken prior to her tattoos, the photographer did a great job of covering them up. Once in America, Sitti Deeba was embarrassed by the tattoos and wanted them removed from her face. Giddi agreed. However, in the process of removing the tattoos, her face became very badly scarred. As a result, Sitti Deeba walked around covered by a black veil to hide her scars and tattoos.

13

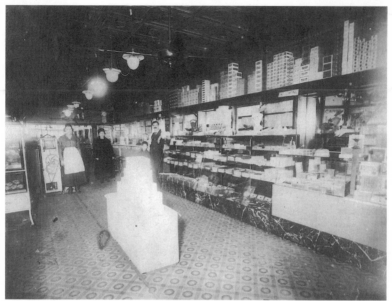

Giddi George's confectionary store in the 1920's in South Brownsville,
Pennsylvania.

Mom was born in South Brownsville – now known as
Brownsville, Pennsylvania after the consolidation in 1933 of
these two boroughs – a mining town outside Pittsburgh where
Polish, Syrian, Russian, and other immigrants flocked to work in
the coal mines. When my grandfather married Sitti Nellie in 1911,
they moved to a lovely home located at 313 Middle Alley in South
Brownsville. Today, the home is no longer there and has been replaced by a parking lot.

My mother's father, Giddi George, was very well-to-do in
South Brownsville. He and Sitti Nellie had five girls (Florence,
Katherine, Olga, Emily, and Virginia) and one son (Alexander).
Katherine, who became my Mom, always said that Giddi George
wanted to name all his children after kings and queens of Russia.
Giddi George was an excellent businessman and owned two confectionery stores. A confectionery store is equivalent to a later day
ice cream parlor and restaurant. Boxes of candy, mounds of
homemade ice cream, and the aroma of Giddi George's famous
hotdogs and hamburgers sizzling on the grill filled the air. The

Bridge and Water Streets in South Brownsville as they looked in the 1920's showing a side view of Giddi George's confectionary store.

Bridge and Water Streets in the late 1800's:
Building Complex established in 1837.

The outside of Giddi's store, now called Fiddle's Confectionery. To the right, a freight train can be seen passing by on its way to the train station.
(Picture dated 2006)

railroad station was only a couple of blocks from one of the confectionery stores. So Giddi would have hot dogs and hamburgers already cooked and waiting for the train to slow down to a crawl as it approached the famous Union Station at 53 Market Street. This daily ritual allowed the train conductor and his railroad workers to jump off the train in front of the confectionery store, grab their already prepared meal still hot off the grill, and get back on a moving car before the train completely passed his store. Oh, what memories Giddi George's children had about their wonderful life in Pennsylvania! In 1918, Giddi George gave one of the stores to his nephew, Fadell Hallal. In 1923, Fadell purchased the building housing his confectionery store. One popular item on the menu that is still a favorite of the customers today is the grilled hot dogs and hamburgers. He claimed his secret was the salt he put on the grill but I think it was the history of the past. That's what has kept the flavor. Oh well, that's an "old wives tale," isn't it?

Giddi George and his family were so generous that he and his relatives Bady, Abe, Michael, Asa, and Hallal built St. Ellien

St. Ellien Syrian Orthodox Church in
Brownsville built in 1917 thanks to the
generosity of Giddi George and his brothers.
The church has the distinction of being the
only one, outside Syria, to be dedicated to St.
Ellien of Homs, Syria who is also often referred
to as St. Julian. *(Picture dated 2006)*

Syrian Orthodox Church, located at 500 Spring Street in
Brownsville. The Church was named after the Eastern Orthodox
Saint Julian (Ellien in Arabic). St. Ellien was formed and fully
chartered on March 31, 1917, but the actual charter was dated and
issued on January 26, 1920. There are only two churches dedicated to Saint Julian: the original Church of St. Julian in Homs,
Syria, and the Church of St. Ellien in Brownsville. What a giving
group of immigrants who came to America to be free of tyranny
and to be able to worship in their own religion. That was what
Giddi George and Sitti Nellie's parents wanted for them, and
they were going to carry on the tradition.

However, when the local economy deteriorated, Giddi George's business declined to such a degree that he could hardly support his family. The poor economy was a mirror image of the poor economy throughout the nation. Giddi George was a businessman and the 1920s and 1930s brought despair to families throughout the United States. The once thriving mining towns were not sheltered. The poverty, lack of jobs, and shortage of money all contributed to a poor economy for the townspeople. Giddi George and Sitti Nellie decided to pack up their family and move to Brooklyn, New York. He thought that when he returned he could sell his property. Many years later on a trip to Brownsville, he found that his property was in foreclosure and he lost everything. In order to keep peace in the family, and not cause bad feelings with his brother, Giddi George did nothing to reclaim his properties.

Giddi George arrived in Brooklyn in 1926 where he rented a house at 454 State Street for one year and then moved down the block to 562 State Street. Mom and her sisters attended P.S. 47 (a girl's public school) and Mom's brother, Alex, attended P.S. 15 (a boy's public school). It was not uncommon at that time to have New York City public schools segregated by sex. In 1928, Mom attended Girls' Commercial High School as a freshman when it opened its doors in the late 1920's. Once again, Mom attended a segregated school. Public high schools such as Bay Ridge High School, Boys High School, Brooklyn Technical High School, and Clara Barton are just a few examples of those built in New York City in the first quarter of the twentieth century which were originally segregated by sex.

The only way I knew about my mother as she grew up was from her older sister, Florence, and younger sisters, Emily and Virginia. Mom only told me how sad she was to leave school and work in a factory. Uncle Alex, Aunt Flo, and Mom were the oldest children and were sent to work. Evidently, Emily and Virginia did not feel the hardships. Therefore, Mom kept her "unselfish" feelings buried inside her heart so that she could help support the family. However, when Aunt Emily and Aunt Virginia would reminisce about my mother, Mom would just smile with a mischievous gleam in her eyes. They called Mom "awiee" which meant strong-willed in Arabic. *Yes*— that was my mother. She was strong-willed and always had to have her own way. Her parents were so frustrated with her in South Brownsville that they sent her to New York City when she was seven to see if her uncles could "tame her." They had to be kidding! No one was able to change Mom's personality.

It turned out that life in New York City was no better than in South Brownsville. Depression hit the nation, leaving Giddi George often without a job and without money to sustain his wife and five children. Mom's sister, Olga, had died when she was in her teens. The truth was never told about how she died but one story goes that she got dizzy on the train station and fell onto the tracks. Another rumor was that she fell in love with a young man that her father didn't approve of and she killed herself. We will never know.

Giddi George had been used to being his own boss in Pennsylvania and not taking orders from anyone. In New York City, it was a different story. He would get one job after the other, but he never stayed long at any of them. It was very hard for him to take orders from a boss. He was his own boss in Pennsylvania – not in New York City. During the Depression, each sister had a domestic chore to perform. Mom's job was to make sure the rooms were neat and clean and the clothes were washed and ironed properly. If her younger sisters did not iron their blouses properly, she would crumple them into a ball and make them iron the blouses all over again. Tough lady, but her sisters learned to respect Katie because she was a hard worker and fulfilled her obligation to bring money and food into the household during the hard times of the 1930s. Mom was very talented as a seamstress and designer of hats – an item that was in demand in the 1920's and 1930's. She established a work ethic that would follow her for the rest of her life.

My father, William Beddy Cury, at his graduation from
Manual Training (which later became John Jay High
School) in Park Slope, Brooklyn, New York. *(1927)*

My parents' families had a common ethnic and religious
bond. Dad boasted about the fact that his parents were of Syrian
ancestry while Mom proudly reminded us that we were of Syrian
and Greek extract. Lebanese was never mentioned by Sitti Nellie.
However, when Aunt Flo reminisced about her family, she re-
called Sitti Nellie referring to the "mountains, you know, over
there in Lebanon." Sitti Nellie was born in Tripoli, a city in present-day Lebanon. In spite of the "Cedars of Lebanon" description
in *The Bible* going as far back as the *Book of Psalms*, no one claimed
that they were Lebanese. At least no one in the generation of my

Sitti Nellie. Sitti Nellie only spoke of her hometown as being a place in Syria.

Unfortunately, when the Depression Era gripped our nation, Mom had to quit high school in 1929 and work in a millinery factory to help the family survive. It is amazing that although she only completed her freshman year at Girls Commercial, she could recall every moment she attended. She learned how to swim in the palatial and sparkling new swimming pool, she climbed the marble staircase leading to the second floor everyday, and she rode the hand-control elevator to the top floor to have lunch. She never—in all her dreams—thought that one of her children would one day work at her beautiful and pristine school which would eventually be called Prospect Heights High School. Little did she know that I would be appointed, in February 1977, as the Assistant Principal of Mathematics. That day was so important—not just for me, but for Mom as well.

For Mom and her family, life in the 1930's was not easy but the family was able to sustain itself. Mom's three sisters (Flo, Emily, and Virginia) and brother (Alex) remained very close. During the Depression Era, all the sisters except Virginia had to go to work. Flo only graduated from eighth grade and Emily graduated from a beauty school after two years of study past eighth grade. Giddi George could not survive the humiliation of the family working while he couldn't hold a job, and on February 24, 1936, he was found dead in his bathroom as a result of a head injury. He would never see his children marry, have his grandchildren play in his lap, or have his wife near him. The family grieved the untimely death of their young father. Sitti Nellie wore black for many years. All the mirrors in the house had to be draped in black. This was customary in a Lebanese or Syrian household. Sitti Nellie and her children mourned the loss of this broken-hearted man. Life had to go on, though, and the children continued to work as a close-knit family to make sure that their mother was taken care of.

Ironically, when Mom was living at 562 State Street, she was only a few blocks away from her future husband's house at 481

Third Street. It was common for relatives to marry within their family. Uncle Galeb (son of Giddi Cury) married Aunt Annie (sister of Sitti Nellie). So, Uncle Galeb and Aunt Annie became my uncle and aunt as well as my great-uncle and great-aunt. They knew Mom's family very well and encouraged my Dad to court her. That is how she met my father and his family. It was not unusual for Syrians to only associate with members from their own ethnic group, but also their own religion. This relationship of socialization, where the same ethnic groups married, was encouraged since Lebanese and Syrians shared the same religion, foods, music, and common interests in America as well as in Lebanon and Syria. One important factor in a union was that the couple not only had to be of the *same* ethnic background but also of the *same* religion. Traditionally, Lebanese and Syrian Antiochian Orthodox rarely married Lebanese and Syrian Catholics and vice versa in our families. Christian immigrants from Syria and Lebanon dominated the exodus from their homelands to America. Very few immigrants were Moslems. Many immigrants to America in the first half of the twentieth century were Christians. As families arrived in America from Lebanon and Syria, they stayed together in specific areas of Brooklyn: Downtown Brooklyn, Atlantic Avenue, Brooklyn Heights, Sunset Park, and Bay Ridge. This was true of other ethnic groups as well.

The years passed quickly as Dad's family socialized with Mom's sisters and brother. Dad's sisters, Rose and Jennie, were very close to all of Mom's sisters. They grew up as "best friends." Aunt Jennie was called our "fun aunt." When she was young, she was just stunning. She loved to sing and dance (as well as flirt). Mom recalls how she would dress up in a red satin dress, her jet black hair shining and held by a beautiful hair clasp in the back. Looking like a movie actress, she would sing, "The Lady in Red." Aunt Jennie would always go up to you and say, "Honey, your Aunt Jennie loves you." And we loved and adored her. It was not a surprise when many years later she married Uncle Frank Abdoo and moved to Neon, Kentucky. Aunt Jennie loved my parents so much that she bestowed upon her brother and sister-in-law, Bill and Katie, the honor of being the godparents for all her children.

Despite the Depression Era, Giddi Cury's family continued to flourish. His clothing factory expanded production and he began to do very well in the retail dry goods business. He was a very wealthy man but also a very strict one. Dad had worked for Giddi Cury upon graduating from Manual Training High School, a prestigious technical school for young men in Park Slope, Brooklyn. Galeb and Tom also worked for their father. Apparently, an argument ensued between Giddi and Uncle Tom. Uncle Tom got mad and left for Kentucky. He was soon followed by Dad. Dad had graduated from Manual Training in Brooklyn in the spring of 1927. He did tell us that he went to Syria after graduating from Manual Training High School and attended "a university." Dad's brother, Galeb, followed them down South and opened up a store in Norton, Virginia.

All three brothers ran "dry goods" stores featuring the finest merchandise in the state of Kentucky. Miners and farmers traveled from all counties to Dad and Uncle Tom's store to buy "what was sold in New York City." They were able to purchase dress suits, fedoras, leather dress shoes, and high fashion clothing for their wives and children. When Dad arrived in the early 1930s, he had his own building where he lived on top of the store. It was a common practice for the owners to live on the floor above their business. A grate was usually located on the top floor so that they could look below to make sure no one robbed the store during non-business hours. I can only speculate that times were bad during the Depression and people were desperate. Business owners had to be careful and so they were vigilant when it came to protecting their assets. As the Curys, Dawahares, and other Lebanese and Syrian families moved into the town – Neon became a place where the coal miners came from all over to purchase goods. Pack peddlers disappeared and retailers took their place. Other Syrian and Lebanese families moved into the area. Sam

My mother and father in front of Charlie Hazen's
Store in Neon, Kentucky. Mom is carrying my
older brother, George Bill. *(c.1939)*

Hush, Frank Abdoo, and the Hazen family were a few of the families that started to build Neon into a hub for trade.

Around 1936, it was time for Dad to get married. Giddi Cury reminded him of this fact. After all, Dad was 27! Dad went back and forth to Brooklyn to socialize with Syrians and Lebanese — one of whom was Katherine, a daughter of the Ellien family and the niece of his sister-in-law, Anastasia, known as Annie. He had his eye on Katie, a feisty young woman and one of the four remaining daughters of George and Nellie Ellien. Katie was not like the rest of her sisters. She was serious, bright, straight-arrowed, and "played by the rules." She didn't smoke like some of her other sisters, always took everything seriously, and didn't flirt with young men. Uncle Galeb had encouraged Dad to go out with his niece, Katie. Dad went back and forth to Kentucky and corresponded with his lovely Katie. At that time, Uncle Galeb's daughters, Rose G. (G for Galeb to differentiate between Rose B. where B stood for Beddy) and Alice, were very close friends with Mom. Why not? The families were separated by only a few blocks from each other in downtown Brooklyn. Dad and Mom began a beautiful courtship. Almost 70 years later, a packet of love letters was found neatly wrapped with a pink ribbon in the right corner of Katie's hope chest. Dad had the best penmanship in his family. He was a romantic and a poet who used flowery words and music to express his love for Katie. There was a song at the time called "Katie" and he used to sing it to her when he was courting her – "KKKKatie" was the love of his life.

Finally, in the early spring of 1936, Dad arrived in Brooklyn– determined to pop the question to Mom. Times were bad since the Depression brought many families to bankruptcy. Not Dad. He was loaded! He carried a money belt swelling with thousands of dollars to buy merchandise for his store when he came up North on his annual buying trips. On one visit that spring, he was traveling with Katie, who was 21, on the subway train when he proposed to her. She objected stating that she couldn't get married until her oldest sister Florence got married first and besides, she was needed to bring income into the family. Dad refused to give up and, in a boisterous voice, announced to everyone in the car that he would pay for the wedding, all the trimmings and more. Mom continued to say, "NO!" She told him that her family didn't have money for a wedding dress. Dad said it was customary for the groom to pay for everything. "Don't worry, Katie, money isn't an issue." She continued to give the excuse that "Flo, my older sister, has to get married first" until the passengers on the train got so frustrated and sick about this young girl's unwillingness to say yes that they yelled out, "Say yes, Katie." "Yes" finally streamed out of her mouth as the passengers cheered! Dad presented her with a two and a half carat diamond which she later proudly pointed out to us, saying how perfect the diamond was. Yes, their love was as perfect as their tangible possessions.

The wedding was held in Giddi Cury's home on Third Street. Dad was so in love with Mom that he bought her wedding dress and her entire trousseau, including six evening gowns which she had to keep changing into during the wedding reception. Each new color was more magnificent than the last. It was helpful that it was customary in the family for the groom to pay for the entire wedding as it was obvious that Mom's family could not afford such a lavish wedding. Yes, Mom had won a prize when she said, "Yes," to this wealthy American. Mom would sing the song, "My Bill," and reminisce about the days with Dad for the next five decades. However, she never shared her intimate feelings about her marriage with any of her children. That was what Katie was about—prim and proper. For all the years I lived with them until I got married, I never heard a passionate sound from their bedroom at night or saw them with intimate apparel. Prim and proper was Katie.

They got married on August 2, 1936 at a gala celebration in Giddi Cury and Sitti Deeba's one-family home at 481 Third Street. Their wedding ceremony was followed by a magnificent reception. It wasn't until very recently that I found out that Sitti Deeba didn't attend the wedding reception but stayed in the kitchen so that no one could see her ugly tattoos. It was said that she was an excellent cook, but that wasn't true. She came from a very wealthy family and didn't have to cook. My cousin, Rose B., told me that although she wasn't a cook, she did know how to bake our ethnic desserts.

The day after the wedding, the happily married couple wasted no time and quickly left New York City heading south to Neon, Kentucky. Mom sadly said her farewells and followed Dad back to the town of Neon in Letcher County—a coal mining area; coal was the main commodity of the state. When Mom reminisced about her first day in Neon, she told us that the streets were not paved, there was no indoor plumbing, and the mining town was right out of Zane Grey's books about the Wild West. On the day of their arrival, they had just missed a gun shooting which resulted in a man's brains dangling outside a saloon. "Oh my God, why did I come to this forsaken town?" She didn't know if she wanted to stay or run away as far as she could. She loved Bill and it wouldn't be proper to leave her husband after less than a month of marriage. Strong-willed, she persevered. As time passed, she grew to love Neon. She missed her sisters and brother, but communicated with them by phone and letters. My older brother, George, and I were born within the first three years of their marriage.

As we grew up in Neon, Dad would sing his beautiful love songs in Arabic as we rode in his car along the winding mountains of Kentucky. Dad would sing in Arabic and translate the song into English. Yes, he was a romantic at heart and always treasured his heritage. I never knew about his fluency in French until I took French in high school and Dad was my tutor. I guess that was the reason I won the French Award at graduation. It was not uncommon for Lebanese and Syrians to be fluent in French, since France dominated the Middle East for decades during the latter part of the nineteenth century and the early twentieth century.

Growing up in the South prevented George and me from learning Arabic. Our parents would speak Arabic to us and although we understood what they said, we would respond in English. We were ashamed to speak anything but English. It was not a smart thing down South to speak a foreign language, especially after World War II. I regret that we did not become completely versed in the Arabic language. My parents held their heads up and spoke Arabic and English. They were both first generation Americans and they wanted to retain their language and heritage. Not us, we understood Arabic but we were too embarrassed to speak it. What would our friends think? That was a mistake, but that was how those times were in the Deep South.

My Aunt Flo and Mom always bragged about Dad's penmanship. In addition, Dad had the innate gift of drawing. I still have

Outside my father's store in Neon, Kentucky. My mother and Sitti Nellie, to her left, walk past Dad's car. Brother, George, is at Mom's side. *(1941)*

proof of his artistic talents: when he closed his department store to attend my wedding, he composed a 20-foot banner in calligraphy stating, "Closed to attend our daughter's wedding." I have preserved the banner because it reminds me of my Dad's talents and love for me. My brothers, George and Bill, inherited the artistic talents of our Dad —but not me!

When George was born in 1937, Sitti Nellie had to rush down to Neon to take care of Mom. Unfortunately, her only child still at home, Virginia, was about to graduate from Girls' Commercial High School. Years later, Aunt Virginia would constantly remind her nephews and nieces that her mother was not able to attend the graduation ceremony since she had to go down South and be with our Mom at the birth of her first grandchild, which was on June 6. In fact, on every delivery of one of her grandchildren, Sitti Nellie would always be there to help her daughters and daughter-in-law, Aunt Jessie. The only problem was when she went to help Katie in the South, it was a long, extended stay. At that time, it was the way of all the Lebanese and Syrian women. It was expected. As women became liberated, the ways changed —but not

My mother and me, at age two, visiting family in
Neon, Kentucky. (1941)

for Sitti Nellie, not at all. She was a special grandmother and
mother to her family. Sitti Nellie continued to maintain the traditions that she learned from her mother and her mother's mother
until her death in 1963. She was always there for her family. That's
what grandmothers were all about. At least that was what my
wonderful Sitti Nellie was all about!

As the years passed in Neon, Kentucky, modern facilities such
as filtered water, paved streets, electricity, indoor toilets, and au-
tomobiles arrived. The Cury family was the first to have every
modern convenience. Although our family was the envy of the
town, we were loved there because Mom and Dad were brought
up in a Christian Lebanese and Syrian-American family to respect and care for those around them. Our religion was Syrian
Orthodox (later to be changed to Antiochian Orthodox) and the

priests taught Dad and Mom and their family the dogma of the Church and we, in turn, were raised in the same faith. The town adored our parents because they cared about the rich and the poor. Our parents represented a connection between the North and the South—a connection that has never been broken. Even today when I visit my hometown in Kentucky, I will always meet someone who will say, "Oh, you are Bill and Katie's daughter. Sure, we remember your family."

The town of Neon was absolutely beautiful. It was nestled in a valley of green where God protected them when the rains came and flooded the valley of Neon. That was Neon's one major problem. Other than that, you were lucky if you were born in Neon; a valley touched by the hands and eyes of God—a place where love and beauty grew amidst the dales of Kentucky.

In 1943 when I was only 4 years old, my older brother, George got into an accident which would have a profound influence on our family for decades to follow. On August 18, which was my birthday, George decided to take a ride on his tricycle, a recent birthday present to him. He met a friend and decided to trade his tricycle for a box of wooden matches. George, dressed in his Tom Mix cowboy suit, went to a creek in the back of our department store and made paper boats to float in the water. He decided to light the boats. Not realizing it, one of the lit paper boats floated towards him and his cowboy suit caught fire. The leather insert protected his privates, but the furry suit lit up in flames resulting in third degree burns from the waist down. They say that four-year-old children do not remember the past as they grow older. Well, I will never forget that day. I wondered what all the screaming was about and why no one was paying any attention to me. I soon found out, and the tragic memories will always be with me. For the next few months, the entire family was with George in the hospital. I never forgot the time when Uncle Tom gave George a crisp, new five dollar bill in the hospital. I cried and asked him where my five dollar bill was. In the 1940s, five dollars was a lot of money. He said, "Don't you fret, honey bun," and right in front of us, he ripped the five dollar bill in half and gave us each half. George could see from my eyes that I was ready to cry. In a very weak voice he said softly, "That's all right, Alice, we can share. " George would always share with me for the rest of his life. Mom nursed George 24-hours-a-day for the following two years. All of Neon rallied together to help this frail six-year-old boy.

Although the drug penicillin was discovered in 1928 by Sir Alexander Fleming, it was never used to kill infections in humans, only in mice at the time. Originally, penicillin was never produced in large quantities; the discovery of life-saving sulfonamide (sulfur drugs) in 1935 kept penicillin away from the forefront for killing germs. However, by the outbreak of World War II in 1939, there was a need to kill the infections sustained on the battlefield. There was soon a need for such a drug in Europe, Asia, and Africa. When the United States entered the War in December of 1941, America needed penicillin to treat its own wounded soldiers. Scientists were able to produce a mold called Penicillium Chrysogenum, discovered on ripe cantaloupes by Mary Hunt from Peoria, Indiana. The valuable drug called penicillin became available in the spring of 1943. It was first tested for military use. By the autumn of 1943, doctors were using the antibiotic in combat zones and limiting use to American and Allied military and to patients with life-threatening infections. One of these patients was George! Isn't there a cliché that "necessity is the mother of invention." The use of penicillin on George's wounds saved his frail body from massive infections. It was amazing how World War II had a wide impact upon the world, including the field of medicine.

Mom had to spend a great deal of time with George. She would recollect to George and me that she could actually see his small veins circulating blood throughout his legs, and because George's body had suffered third degree burns, he had to be very careful he didn't get an infection not only during his childhood, but throughout his adult life. I rarely left George's bedside. When he started to walk, I followed him everywhere. I was his shadow. The doctors predicted that George's growth would be stunted. That did not happen. Mom read to George incessantly in his hospital bed at home for over a year. I would lie at the foot of his bed and listen as Mom took George and me into the world of fantasy and adventure. George grew up to be a handsome and a very bright young man of six feet. He was a scholar and I followed in his footsteps. This had a lot to do with the training from our mother—a woman who had only nine years of formal schooling.

I can remember the hardships and sickness surrounding our household in my childhood. My mother made a vow to God that since he saved George, she would make sure that not one impoverished family who entered Cury's Department Store would go unclothed. She told us this story and lived to fulfill her vows until she had to stop work at the age of 78 because of Alzheimer's disease. She and Dad were so thankful that God had spared their son.

One thing that remains among my earliest memories took place when I was 5 years old (a year after George got burned) I had my tonsils removed. It was 1944 and the doctors in the United States were losing too many children in the operating room due to the use of anesthesia while removing their tonsils. But Alice had to have those infected tonsils removed! So, I was dressed up and had a red patent leather pocketbook full of brand new shiny nickels to pay the doctor for making me better. (Little did I know that I was about to be frightened out of my wits.) Mom took me into a white and shiny room with metal beds and chairs. A doctor and a nurse started to speak to me. I was going to pay them for taking out my tonsils. Can one imagine that a 5 year-old can describe the operating room on the day that her tonsils were removed! I was strapped into a cold metal chair with a circular seat. Everything was clean and white in the room. I soon kicked the nurse as the doctor was placing a white, funny looking gun into my mouth to clip my first tonsil. Mom told me many years later that the nurse still had a permanent bruise on her leg from me. I got the doctor so upset that he left a partial piece of the second tonsil in my mouth. It was not until my early 40s that I saw a similar surgical "gun" used to remove tonsils on television. It was at that moment that the memory of the ordeal returned to me. Well, this tortuous technique didn't lose any children in the 1940s, but what a terrible way to treat little girls and boys!

One other incident that I did not remember, but Mom told me many years later, was when I was 6 years old. My first grade teacher was so upset to always listen to me say, "I can't do this" and, "I can't do that." She decided to write the word **CAN'T** on a piece of paper and take it to the back of the school with the entire class. She made me dig a hole and bury the paper. She was tired of me losing my confidence and this is how she was going to teach me a lesson. I wish I could see her today to thank her for helping me to never give up. I didn't remember this event, but Mom would always remind me about it when I had a problem. For the first two years of George's sickness, I lost the attention of my parents since they needed to focus on George. During this time, I was in the shadows with Mom taking care of George. I lost confidence in myself as a 6-year-old. Mom was going to make sure that George's accident was not going to affect her second born . . . . **never say can't, never say can't, never say can't.**

Chapter II

Moving

Although Mom and Dad did everything for George and although the small town of Neon had rallied behind George and our family, the doctors told our parents that they had to go to Florida so that George could take advantage of the sunshine and the salty air. George looked like a refugee. He was frail and hardly gaining weight in spite of the fact that he was getting taller. In addition, Dad realized that Neon was not a place to raise his family. It was constantly damp from the floods that annually hit the valley and was not healthy for Dad's rheumatism. Business was excellent but it wouldn't continue to be as good. Dad had warned Neon's mayor and city council that they should be careful to moderate the state's plans for building a new super highway that could by-pass their beautiful town. If plans were passed in the state capitol that would result in a modern road bypassing the town, Neon would soon be a ghost town. Dad was a visionary as well as a great businessman. But his words of wisdom fell on deaf ears and, many decades later, the newly built highway did indeed by-pass Neon with the result that Neon quickly became a town with the largest number of welfare families in the state of Kentucky. Businesses left and as of today, only a few of the original families remain. Keep in mind that one business did thrive—coal mining. Black lung was a death wish for the miners, but coal was a major commodity of the state and of the nation.

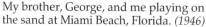

My brother, George, and me playing on
the sand at Miami Beach, Florida. *(1946)*

My mother, Katie, (left) with her cousin,
Alice, (right) in Neon, Kentucky. *(1946)*

It was at this point that reality started to set in with Dad and
Mom. They were going to leave their home in Neon. Dad's sister
(Jennie) and his brothers (Galeb and Tom) were very sad to see
our family go. Uncle Galeb and his wife, Aunt Annie, along with
their daughter, Cousin Alice, decided to take a vacation with us.
So, we all packed up and took off to Florida by car in February of
1946. Dad had sold his business. In early 1946, we were going to
take a long vacation to the Sunshine State of Florida. On the way
down to Florida, we had to stop at many rest points and spend
the night. Little did we know that George was collecting all the
tips that we left at the restaurants where we dined. When we arrived in Miami Beach, George proudly pulled out bills and coins
and told Dad, "Look at all the money I saved for you, Daddy. You
forgot it at every restaurant." Dad and Mom didn't know what to
do. But for sure they weren't going to return to the same restaurants on the way back North!

George finally started to gain weight. We all had a wonderful time in Miami Beach. We played on the beach, swam in the salt water, and laughed and laughed and laughed. There was one "fishy story" that would go down in the Curys' books forever. Here's how it goes. Dad and Uncle Galeb loved to eat fresh fish. In New York City, where they grew up, fresh fish was common but Kentucky was landlocked and as a result they could only buy frozen fish in the supermarkets. Therefore, Uncle Galeb and Dad would go fishing every day in Florida. They spent hundreds of dollars renting a boat. Every day, they returned with a large catch of fresh fish. Mom and Aunt Annie cooked the fresh catch and Dad and Uncle Galeb would boast about their fishing skills. The fish stories got longer and the amount of fish increased each day. I can still smell the red snapper broiling while Aunt Annie and Mom made the most delicious Lebanese garnish called "Taratour." Taratour was made out of sesame seed paste called tahini, garlic, and lemon juice, and is still used today. It was not until the end of the trip that Mom and Aunt Annie caught Dad and his brother in the act. The real story was that they were not successful fishing the first day. They spent a lot of money on the fishing boat and caught no fish. So, when they docked at the fishing pier, they purchased another fisherman's catch and came home bragging it was theirs. This was to be a family joke for decades. They almost "pulled the scales,"—oh, I mean "pulled the wool"—over their wives' eyes.

The two months we spent in Florida did a world of good for George. The sunshine, salty air and water, as well as fresh orange juice, were just what the doctor ordered. Since George's health improved so much, Dad and Mom felt we were ready to move to Brooklyn, New York. Uncle Galeb and Aunt Annie were very sad but they knew that the family needed a change. Uncle Galeb and Aunt Annie headed back to Kentucky. Our parents decided to settle in a community called Bay Ridge located in the borough of Brooklyn in New York City. Apparently, a large group of

Lebanese and Syrian Christian immigrants had settled in this beautiful community along the Narrows Bay.

Bay Ridge is an area of Brooklyn that includes the old boundaries of New Utrecht and land formerly known as Yellow Hook. Apparently in December of 1853, the townspeople of Yellow Hook met to discuss changing the name. Many felt that Yellow Hook was not an appropriate name because they did not want it to be associated with the dreaded disease, Yellow Fever. James Weir, a florist at the time, suggested the name "Bay Ridge." The townspeople, without a formal council vote or another government agency, approved the change and Yellow Hook became Bay Ridge. Bay Ridge was the area bounded on the east by 4th Avenue, on the west by the Bay, on the north by 69th Street and on the south by the Narrows.

During the nineteenth and early twentieth centuries, wealthy businessmen and politicians built stately mansions in Bay Ridge, among them the Van Brunt Mansion (later the Crescent Club, followed by Fort Hamilton High School); the Henry C. Murphy Mansion; the David C. Bennett Mansion (on the corner of 79th Street and 4th Avenue); the William R. Bennett Mansion (on the corner of 79th Street through to Third Avenue); The Farrell House (125 95th Street); and the J. Remsen Bennett Mansion (on the south corner of 77th Street). The Farrell House still remains and is an official landmark. E.W. Bliss purchased the Henry C. Murphy estate with additional lands totaling 65 acres in Bay Ridge. Bliss built an observatory tower of granite on the property. The tower and his mansion are no longer standing. However, part of the property is Owl's Head Park and became public in the 1920's. The William R. Bennett mansion was torn down in 1926 and is presently the site of apartments which were built in the late 1920's.

At the tip of Bay Ridge, on the corner of 101st Street and 4th Avenue in the John Paul Jones Park, can be found an original Civil War-era cannon, called the Rodman gun, complete with cannon balls. The cannon weighs about 58 tons, and each of its 20-inch shots on display there weighs just over 1000 pounds. Rodman guns were designed by a Union artilleryman, Thomas Jackson Rodman, who used a new technology to make these cannons much stronger than their predecessors. They were intended to be mounted on seacoast fortifications and that is how one of them ended up in Bay Ridge. Apparently, it was only used once, in 1864, when soldiers at nearby Fort Hamilton tested it out. Now it overlooks the Verrazano Bridge to Staten Island.

The subway linking Bay Ridge to Chambers Street in lower Manhattan was opened in 1916. As people flocked to Bay Ridge, many of the area's grand houses were torn down to make room for areas such as Ridge Boulevard, Shore Road, and Narrows Avenue. Apartment houses sprung up throughout Bay Ridge. Brick and stucco homes replaced homesteads and farms. Churches of all denominations sprung up. Bay Ridge was rapidly changing. Some of the famous estate owners such as Mackay (Mackay Place) now have streets named after them. Schools such as P.S. 170, P.S. 185, P.S. 102, and P.S. 104 opened their doors to the public. Victory Memorial Hospital was founded in 1900 and served the Bay Ridge/Dyker Heights community for just over one hundred years before filing for bankruptcy, and closing down in 2008. SUNY Medical Center has taken over the Emergency Room facilities, while a nursing home was established in the remainder of the hospital facilities. When the Belt Parkway was completed in 1940, it brought newcomers from all over the city to settle in Bay Ridge. It also encouraged the development of Long Island suburbia, and it played a significant part in the development of Staten Island. However, this latter change did not come to fruition until 1964 with the linking of Bay Ridge and the Belt Parkway with Staten Island. In the meantime, the 69th Street Ferry shuttled people and cars between the two boroughs. Dad and Mom were use to owning their own house. So in the spring of 1946, they decided to purchase a lovely detached home located at 78 88th Street in Bay Ridge.

George and I attended P.S. 185 on the corner of 86th Street and Ridge Boulevard. The school was located across the broad street

My father, William Beddy Cury, with my older
brother, George Bill, and me in front of our new
home at 78 88th Street in Bay Ridge, Brooklyn.
(1946)

from the Kaufman Orphanage. By this time, the public high
schools and elementary schools were co-educational. Dad invested in the stock market and bought a great deal of military sur-
plus called "job lots." Mom took George and me to the wading
pool and sprinklers located at the public park on Oliver Street
and Shore Road. We had never seen parks with cement, water-
works, see-saws, and monkey bars. What a treat from rural Kentucky! It was so much fun being with our family in Bay Ridge.
Mom had more time to give to Dad since George was feeling
better and needed less medical attention. Our brother, William
(nicknamed Willie), was born September 16, 1947. Uncle Alex's
wife, Aunt Jessie, was a favorite aunt and sister-in-law to Mom.
She prepared the baby's crib with beautiful blue ribbons, a soft

blue blanket, and all the toiletries that Mom needed for Willie. George and I rushed home the day Mom and Dad brought Willie home. He was our beautiful baby brother! He was born with a crop of brown hair and the most beautiful blue eyes, which soon changed to brown like Mom's. The first thing I headed for after seeing Willie was the refrigerator to look for baby food. Alas, no baby food! I soon found out that baby food was not to be a part of Willie's diet for quite a while. I was so disappointed.

Dad was not very happy living in Bay Ridge. He missed his brothers in Kentucky and was not too thrilled dealing with "job lot surpluses" from World War II. So after two years, he decided to move back to Kentucky, but this time he wanted to settle in Prestonsburg where he could be near his brother, Galeb. On December 26, 1947, New York City experienced one of its worst blizzards of the century. It lasted two days but did not stop Dad and Mom from loading the family car with all their children and suitcases and heading back to Kentucky. We followed the moving van through snow and sleet. We were on our way to Prestonsburg, Kentucky, approximately 900 miles away.

Prestonsburg was located in Floyd County about 80 miles southeast of Neon and 13 miles north of Paintsville, Kentucky—the town where Uncle Galeb lived. Dad couldn't wait until he got there ...but Mom was not very happy, as all her family lived in Brooklyn. Nonetheless, she loved Dad and was willing to follow him once again.

Dad purchased a large house with a huge backyard. Looking out to the right of the back yard was a 50 ft. trellis of grapevines. Now Mom would have no trouble cooking stuffed grape leaves for us, a Lebanese and Syrian delicacy. Well, you know who was going to pick those grape leaves? Mom had enough leaves to freeze for the winter and to share with Uncle Galeb and Aunt Annie.

Uncle Tom's red brick dry goods building in Neon, Kentucky had his name, "THOS. B. CURY," and the year it was built, "1947," embedded in a cement plaque on the outside. His name was still on top of that building when I visited the town almost forty-eight years later. Unfortunately, the building had deteriorated so badly that it will probably be torn down in the coming years. Dad also had his own store built the same year but his was located in Prestonsburg where we had settled after moving from Bay Ridge.

When Dad was having his store built, the Mayor sent a delegation to speak to him. They had heard Mom and Dad speak a "foreign language." It was Arabic and, of course, in

The name on the stone insert shown here is my uncle, Thomas Beddy (Thos. B.) Cury. He owned this building in Neon, Kentucky which he built in 1947 for his dry goods store. *(2006)*

the South, one only spoke English. There were no blacks (back then the word used in the South was "Coloreds"), Catholics, or Jews who lived in the town. The town officials came to Dad and told him that he had to leave. When Dad questioned them, they said that they did not want any Jews living in their town. Dad explained that he was not Jewish, but a Syrian-American Christian. They told him that was fine. "Assyrians were welcome." We laughed, but we let them get away with Assyrians and Syrians. My parents laughed about it for years to come, how parochial and prejudiced were Southerners. This was just one example of the overt prejudice which permeated the South during the period prior to the Civil Rights Movement in the 1960s. The townspeople soon accepted us Northerners. Dad had built a beautiful store with name brands such as Bostonian Shoes, Cole of California Sports Wear, Munsingwear, Vitality Shoes, and Botany 500 suits. The local officials were hesitant when Dad and Mom arrived in late December of 1947, but they soon noticed as the years passed how Dad and Mom's philanthropic attitude benefited the town. The Curys became permanent fixtures in Eastern Kentucky.

Dad was closest to his brother Galeb. Galeb and Annie lived only 13 miles away from Prestonsburg in a small town called Paintsville. They were very close to Dad going as far back as the first year of their marriage in 1911 when Dad was just 2 years old. They were newlyweds and pretended to be parents to our father. Dad used to tell us how Annie and Galeb (14 years older than Dad) would tuck Dad into bed between them at night. They adored Dad as their son, and Galeb was more of a father to Dad than his own father. Annie became a real mom to Dad as well. She was not only my aunt on my father's side, as Galeb's wife, but she was also my great-aunt on my mother's side, as my Sitti Nellie's sister, Anastasia (Annie). Aunt Annie had migrated to America in 1910 with Sitti Nellie and her family. Our father liked the "double relationship" and cherished Galeb and Annie. They had a son – who of course was called Beddy G.— the "G" stood for Galeb. There was a Beddy born to Dad's sister, Mary, and a Beddy T. born to Dad's brother, Tom. No matter what Beddy G. did, he was <u>never</u> wrong. Beddy G. even became our parents' best man at their wedding. Dad had a very favorite place in his heart for him.

When Willie was a toddler, it would take hours for him to fall asleep. We remember Mom creeping down the stairs when it appeared that Willie was sleeping. George and I could hear the creaks of the floors as she descended each step. "Careful, Katie, don't wake up Willie," we whispered quietly under our sheets. We shuddered with fear that Willie would hear her movements down the staircase. Would those wooden steps ever stop their incessant noise? When she finally slid down to the last step and Willie heard that last creak from the planks of the staircase steps, he knew Mom was downstairs. A piercing noise vibrated in our ears as Willie screamed for his Mommy. Without complaining, Mom would turn around and go back to Willie's room for

My parents, Katie and William Beddy,
alongside my brother, George, outside our
home in Prestonsburg, Kentucky. Younger
brother, Willie, and I are in front. *(1948)*

another bedtime story. When she finally got him to sleep, Uncle Galeb, who cherished Willie, often teased Mom by driving 13 miles from Paintsville to wake Willie up and immediately drive back leaving the hysterical baby crying at the top of the staircase. Uncle Galeb begged Mom and Dad to give Willie to them. He wanted Willie as a son, not a nephew. Dad's sister, Thana, who was childless also begged to take Willie. She was even willing to offer money for him. Mom was crazed and wouldn't think about it. Willie was her child and not Galeb's or Thana's. Finally, Aunt Thana and Uncle Galeb got the message, "No Deal!"

The next few years in Prestonsburg were priceless. We grew up in a town with a population of 2,000. The townspeople worked for six days during the week. However, the seventh day was truly the Sabbath day. Families went to church, ate their Sunday dinner, and did everything as a family. There was no such thing as "getting a baby-sitter." The entire family went or no

Another family picture from
Prestonsburg, Kentucky. Back row,
standing L to R: Me, holding younger
brother, Willie, by the arms; my cousins,
Edward and Robert Bittar; and my older
brother, George. Crouching in front is
my cousin, Donald Bittar. *(1948)*

one went! We lived, dined, and traveled as a family. George and I had fun having a baby brother so much younger: George was 14, I was 12, and Willie was 4. Willie brought happiness and joy to our childhood and adolescent years. He helped make up for a significant period of unhappiness while Mom devoted so many years in nursing George back to health. So, now it was time to have fun with our beautiful baby brother, Willie!! That's why until today, I have a very special place in my heart for Willie, now known as Bill after Dad died in 1968.

Whenever Willie was sick, we knew it. He would take his little red wicker rocker, place it on top of the furnace grate and drink a glass of cold milk. "Oops . . . . Call the doctor, Willie is going to come down with a temperature." And he did. Willie soon earned the name of "Dennis the Menace." Oops, I mean "Willie the

A family portrait of the three of us, oldest to youngest:
(L to R) George, me, and Willie. *(1953)*

Menace." Willie was different from George and me. He was willing to always take chances, was creative, and thought "outside the box." That's probably why Willie was the financial success of the family later on in life.

One day, when Willie was 6, he disappeared. The entire town searched high and low. Police, firemen, neighbors, and employees from the store—everyone searched for Willie. About 6:30 in the evening, Mom decided to lie down a few minutes. She headed for her bedroom and collapsed onto the bed. Before she put her head on the pillow, she heard a slurping noise. "Slurp, slurp, slurp." Mom would recall the sounds for years to come. She looked under her dressing table and—lo and behold—there was Willie finishing off a pound jar of Elizabeth Arden cold cream. You couldn't scold him because he had these big brown eyes that would melt you away.

Another occasion when Willie tried Dad and Mom's patience was when he set Mom's deodorant stick on fire. This happened in their bedroom. He thought it was a candle. He got scared and must have thrown the lit deodorant stick onto the oriental carpet adjacent to their bed. Willie called my brother, George, who was at the store, and said that there was a fire in the bedroom. George immediately called the Fire Department. Smelling the fire, I ran up the stairs and found Mom sitting on a couch in the foyer crying hysterically, "Not another son; not another fire..." During her hysterics, I ran to the bathtub and soaked a large Turkish bath towel. Rushing past Mom who was still hysterical in the hallway, I ran into the bedroom and doused the fire. Her solid mahogany bed was partially damaged along with the oriental rug. However, all was well. Material things could be replaced. We had learned that lesson from George's accident. Neither her second son nor anyone else in the family was burned like her George had been many years ago. And Willie never did that again!

Mom missed her sisters so Dad sent her and Willie to New York City for a visit when Willie was 7. Mom was the wealthiest of all the sisters and was very generous. She decided to treat Emily, Flo, and Virginia to a show at Radio City Music Hall. They would see a movie as well as watch the famous Radio City Rockettes. Of course, they took Willie with them. Each sister had a 30-minute baby-sitting responsibility to take care of Willie and his needs (candy, bathroom or just supervising him as he explored the lobby). Aunt Flo told Mom to give Willie a location in case he got lost. At this point, my mother was exhausted with having Willie on her trip to New York City, so she responded to her sister's suggestion with a little twinkle in her eyes, "Do I have to?" Well, Aunt Flo told us many years later that by the time the movie and stage show were over at Radio City Music Hall, the entire front and back rows were completely empty. Who wanted to sit next to that spoiled boy? He was the baby of the family and was our "Willie the Menace" for many years.

There were good times too. On a typical Saturday afternoon, Dad would give George and me a quarter each to take Willie to the Saturday matinee. The tickets for us ran ten cents each and

Willie was free. It was a double show plus the usual weekly serial show featuring Captain Marvel or "The Three Stooges." The film was usually *Abbott and Costello Meet the Werewolf* or another film from our favorite comedy team. We had enough money for the tickets plus food money for Willie: candy bars, popcorn, soda pop, ice cream—the usual. George and I would buy one miniature fruit pie—for it was only a nickel—and split it between the three of us. We had a feast. Of course, we had to see the movies twice since we took turns taking Willie to the candy counter, then to the bathroom, then back to the candy counter, then back to the bathroom . . . . We followed standard procedures. We pretended we were his parents. It was fun. George was 16 and I was 14. We looked mature for our age and Willie looked like our son. "Oh, those were the days!" George was of dating age and many of the teenagers in the town were slowly getting pregnant. When I was asked out for a date at 14, Dad said, "That's it, Katie. I want the children to date Syrians and they must be Syrian Orthodox." This was almost impossible in Kentucky which was predominantly Protestant and non-Syrian with the exception of our relatives and friends who lived in Kentucky, Virginia, and West Virginia. No one understood what our religion was. We attended Sunday services at the Presbyterian Church adjacent to our home. The Presbyterians didn't understand what Syrian Orthodoxy was or the fact that we were completely submerged into water when we were less than a year old. The pastor kept trying to convince our parents to baptize us. Dad and Mom got so frustrated that they told him that we were the same religion as the Greek Orthodox. That must have been enough to convince the pastor to stop asking our parents to have us baptized.

Dad and Mom were highly respected in both towns since they had "an eastern department store" with all the fashionable styles from the North and West. They were honorable and kind to their customers and tried to do the very best for them and the town.

However, I knew Dad and Mom wanted us to be around our family and close to those of our nationality and religion. He decided to take a trip to New York and took me with him. He and I traveled by train to New York City to pick out an apartment. Uncle Alex, Mom's only brother, picked us up in his yellow, medallion cab and we headed for Bay Ridge once again!

We rented the second floor of the O'Connor's two-family house at 7209 Narrows Avenue. We headed back to Prestonsburg where the town was shocked to hear that the Curys were leaving. We had lived in Prestonsburg for six years. George and I had so many farewell parties.

I will never forget what one of my best friends, Rose, said to me before we left. We had just finished ninth grade and Mom gave a party for my friends and me. "Well, Alice, now I won't have to worry about you competing with me for valedictorian when we graduate high school." I was hurt by the thoughtlessness of her words. Years later, when I returned for a 25-year reunion in 1982, I learned that Rose had become very sick. She died in 2000 without me ever seeing her since childhood yet she will always remain a childhood friend and share a special place in my heart . . . Other friends of mine included Toy Anne, Helen, and Phyllis. We still stay in touch with each other. I do know that family values, love for family, and being good to others were values instilled in us from our parents, family, and the way our parents treated people in the small towns of Prestonsburg and Neon.

I was going to miss the girls I grew up with, as well as my teachers. But it was time to leave. We said our goodbyes to our cousins: Martha, Frankie, Lloyd, and Tommy Abdoo; Tommy and Beddy T. Cury; and to our aunts and uncles: Uncle Frank Abdoo (Aunt Jennie's wonderful husband), Uncle Tom, Uncle Galeb and Aunt Annie who were part of our extended family. It was a sad farewell and the very last time that I would see many of my aunts and uncles until their deaths.

We packed up all our belongings and shipped the furniture in a van back to Bay Ridge in Brooklyn. The only problem was that Dad had not sold the house. On the day we were leaving with the car packed for traveling, Mr. Parsley, our neighbor across the street, came out with $10,000 in cash and purchased our house on the spot. Many decades later, I learned that he gave the house to his granddaughter, Sarah Parsley. Well, we were on our way back to Brooklyn.

Chapter III

Growing up in Brooklyn

D ad parked his brand new 1954 white Cadillac outside the O'Connor's two-family house. The movers were waiting for us. We were so excited—a new city, a new house, a new place to start another chapter in the life of the Cury family. Our happiness did not last too long because while the movers were emptying the van, we heard a fire alarm go off in the street. Our bubble of joy and contentment quickly burst. Everything was happening so fast and all of a sudden, the movers were rushing Willie and Uncle Alex's son, Georgie, up the stairs of our new apartment. We didn't know what the movers were telling Mom and Uncle Alex's wife, Aunt Jessie, but before we knew it, Mom and Aunt Jessie quickly undressed Willie and Georgie and plunged them into the bathtub. Flying down the stairs, the movers quickly blocked the front entrance of the house with our couch. During this frightening episode, Mom started to cry. Aunt Jessie was used to incidents like this because she was a New Yorker. But Mom and the rest of us were not. We were so scared that the police would arrive any minute and take Willie to the police station. The movers were from our hometown of Prestonsburg and were going to make sure that the Cury family didn't get into any trouble. After all,

Dad and Willie stand together in front of Dad's new white Cadillac parked outside our home at 157 83rd Street in Bay Ridge, Brooklyn. *(1954)*

they were Kentuckians and Kentuckians stuck together. I will never forget how kind they were to our parents. Willie told Mom that he thought the fire alarm box was a giant can opener and pulled the handle. It would not only have been a $500 fine, but Willie could have jeopardized the life of another family in case of a real fire. The only fear traveling through my mind at that time was that we were not going to be at peace in this big city. Why did our parents move us from the safe and secure environment of Kentucky? Wasn't Kentucky called "Home Sweet Home." Now, George and I trembled with fear that New York City would present our family with serious problems. Well, our fears dissipated as time passed and Brooklyn did indeed become a second home to us.

We enjoyed our apartment but we were used to owning our own home. The O'Connors were very warm towards us. Mom would bake incessantly. Mrs. O'Connor and their family enjoyed the "yummies." Their son, John, loved grape leaves and our ethnic desserts. The O'Connors made our life easier those first few months in the big city in many ways. Dad recently purchased a Cadillac. At first, Dad kept his Cadillac in a public garage – until the night attendant decided to use it for a date. The next day, Dad found the car outside our apartment with the front banged up like an accordion. Dad was so furious. Needless to say, that was the last time he used the garage. Mr. O'Connor told Dad he could keep his Cadillac in front of his house from now on.

We attended Church on a weekly basis. St. Mary's Church was located two blocks away from our new home. The Church school consisted of over 350 students. George got involved in scouting and I became a fifth grade Sunday school teacher. I couldn't wait to practice teaching.

Dad and Mom shopped around and soon found a beautiful five-bedroom Tudor house at 157 83rd Street, right down the block from our high school. The school song clearly depicted Fort Hamilton High School as the "school along the Bay." The high school was built on the land of the famous Crescent Athletic Club facing the Narrows Bay. The club was known for its excellent tennis courts, glass enclosed dining room, boathouse, and area for athletic competitions in football, bocce, lacrosse, baseball and rowing. The City purchased the building and the property behind it where the famous team players conducted their competitions. The school finally got its name on June 21, 1939 as "Fort Hamilton High School."

The City had to promise that the newly built high school and the City's Parks Department would share equal ownership. The school used the athletic field until dusk during the school week and it returned to the Parks Department after dusk, on weekends, and during the summer. The Parks Department had the responsibility of maintaining the athletic field. New York City's Mayor, Fiorello H. LaGuardia, laid the cornerstone for Fort Hamilton High School on September 23, 1940 and the school opened its doors to the community on September 8, 1941, with a faculty of 130 teachers.

Architect, Eric Kebbon, wanted his building to be the first one visible by all incoming ocean liners. Therefore, he designed a semi-monumental building, constructed with red brick and trimmed with limestone. He had a dominating tower mounted on the top, with six majestic white pillars supporting a canopy roof over the entrance. Somehow or another, the architect reversed the front with the back facades of the school building. The majestic staircase facing Shore Road was indeed the back entrance of the building. Even today when visitors pass the school, they are astonished to see that the front looks as if it should be the back.

The tower housed four 300-watt lights which lit up at night. The tower was to be used for navigational purposes by the ships entering the harbor and was to be visible at all times. As far as I can remember, the tower was very rarely lit and for sure not lit during World War II.

Upon our arrival in 1954, the school was still relatively new and was considered a school of choice for the neighborhood. You could imagine that the school was a college surrounded by a majestic campus. It overlooked the Verrazano-Narrows waterway at the lower end of New York Bay. Its tower glistened when the sunlight hit the windows. The back of the school facing the water was surrounded by a border of Magnolia blossom trees during the spring. The blossoms would hover over the school's wrought iron gate like a giant white and pink umbrella, while the gate wrapped around the school like a belt of authority, offering protection for all who remained within its perimeter. I have always said that Fort Hamilton High School's majestic building, which really does give it the appearance of a college campus, plus the beauty of the Narrows provided a calming and serene atmosphere for the student body.

George and I were disappointed that Fort Hamilton High School did not have a football team or marching band as so many of our schools did in Kentucky. Nevertheless, we worked hard and achieved excellence throughout our high school years.

George and I were registered at the pristine school for eleventh and tenth grade, respectively. To our dismay, the Guidance Department at our new high school decided to lower the A+'s and A's that we received in the Kentucky school system because "the education in Kentucky was not the same quality as the education in New York City." I will never forget those words. I wanted to be a teacher one day and hoped that this situation would never happen to my students. We soon surprised the school and scored 100's on many of our New York State Regents Examinations. One funny incident happened when George and I took the Geometry Regents in the same room. George sat in front of me. George scored 100 on the Regents and I scored 98. My geometry teacher, Mrs. Edith Westerburg, wanted to see why I lost two points. To her surprise, she discovered that I had not missed the question and changed my mark to 100. Our scholarship was not inflated. Absolutely not! George and I were very upset to see that they had to lower our "inflated" marks from down South. The administrators at Fort Hamilton High School who felt that we had an inferior education in Kentucky were dead wrong and George and I proved it in the following years.

We joined many organizations at Fort Hamilton High School. George was active in sports as well as participating in various clubs, and I was also active in clubs and church activities. We had great times growing up in Bay Ridge. I can remember renting bikes at the bike shop on 69th Street with my friends. We used the bicycle path along Shore Road and rode from 69th Street to 100th Street and back. George and I attended school plays, participated in the St. Mary's Church youth organization called, "The Acolytes," and attended SOYO (Syrian Orthodox Youth Organization) Regional Conferences. Yes, we had a wonderful time associating with our friends, especially our friends who attended our church. It was not uncommon for me to get home in the late afternoon or on a Saturday afternoon and find George, Don Shofi, George (Buzzie) Abouselman, and Ronnie Tadross playing Whist. Mom would be baking Syrian and Lebanese sweets called

My brother, George, wearing his graduation gown as the FHHS valedictorian for the Class of 1956.

Ghraybeh (shortbread sugar cookies) and *Maamool* (walnut-filled cookies). As soon as they came out of the oven, George's card group would polish them off with a cold glass of milk. Mom never complained. That's what made a home—a place for the friends of her children to come and socialize and, of course, to eat. When I would complain, she would respond with "that's all right, Alice, I can bake another batch." Yes, growing up in Bay Ridge around all our school friends and relatives was like heaven. There is a book called *A Tree Grows in Brooklyn*. Well, there is also a place called *A Family Grows in Brooklyn*.

Our teen years flew by so quickly. In 1956, George graduated as Valedictorian of Fort Hamilton High School and I followed him as fifth in my graduating class in 1957, achieving an overall average of 95.6. We were both members of Arista, the national honor society, and were the recipients of many awards at graduation. I was particularly proud of receiving the Mathematics,

(Photo courtesy Michael A. D'Ambrosio FHHS Promotional Brochure 1990-91)

In all its majesty, Fort Hamilton High School stands facing the Narrows Bay. Its beauty radiates from the breathtaking magnolia trees in full blossom each spring. Its wrought iron gate wraps around the school like a belt of authority. Its tower stands above reaching out to the sky, while the perpetual clock keeps time for all to watch.

"To look, to see, to learn and to know that time never stops for all who enter. To reach for the gold and never accept less. To have the desire to be the very best."

Never Say You Can't ...Never Say You Can't...

Chemistry, and French Awards at graduation. It was a "no-no" for a young woman at that time to achieve accolades in science and mathematics and I knew the boys were envious of me. Why? Some of my competitors who were boys were actually upset that I received the Math award. Ronnie was one of my friends who came up to me and laughed. "You amaze me, Alice. Boys, not girls, are expected to excel in math." Another friend, Don, drew a picture of me with a point on the top of my head. He thought that was funny, but I didn't. Isn't this attitude still prevalent in our education system today? Well, educators should get over it and realize that it is not about the battle of the sexes but the battle of the minds.

Other classmates who are still close to me today are Vivian and Rose. I met Vivian at P.S. 185 when our family originally came to Brooklyn. We lost touch with each other for a while, but when I arrived as a sophomore at Fort Hamilton High School in 1954, Vivian and I simultaneously spotted each other on the second floor of the school. We hugged each other and started to reminisce about our childhood. One of my very best friends was Elsa Anderson. We kept in touch with each other for the first few years of our undergraduate years. However, as the years passed, Elsa and I went our own way. It was not until almost fifty years later that we reunited. My father once said that you can count your true friends on one hand. Well, one of those friends is Elsa. Elsa fell in love with Richard, married, and had two sons. By a miracle, we have revived our friendship. One thing is sure, I will never lose contact with her again.

My Aunt Flo's daughters, Marian and Regina, both attended Fort Hamilton High School. Regina moved away but my cousin Marian is always around giving to her family, her community, and her church. While living in Bay Ridge, the family grew very close to Rose G. and her wonderful husband, Anthony Bittar. They had a set of twins, Donald and Robert, followed by Edward. All three boys attended Fort Hamilton High School. Cousin Rose G. often reminisced about how she met her Anthony. Anthony had gone to my Sitti Nellie's house to pick up his mother and sister who were attending a bridal shower for my mother. When he arrived, he saw Rose G., a beautiful blonde and blue-eyed girl, singing on the front porch. He went up to her and asked, "Can you sing tenor?" She replied, "Of course." He left and quickly returned with his guitar and they played and sang together. A week later, Rose G. went to Anthony's ice cream parlor and drugstore located at 5101 6th Street in Sunset Park and had a dish of ice cream. An important ingredient of the ice cream was Arabic gum. Since the ice cream was made in Brooklyn, its name took the title as Syrian ice cream. When asking Rose G. about her Anthony over six decades later, she replied, "Anthony was a very 'gentle' man." Yes, I would agree with that. He would always address me when I was a teenager as his "peaches and cream."

A feeling of remorse comes upon Rose when she reminisces about her Anthony. Rose still has the bench seat that she sat on when she first went to Anthony's ice cream parlor and pharmacy. Even in her sadness when she talks about her Anthony, she proudly adds that "Anthony's pharmacy was the first in Brooklyn run by a Syrian who spoke Arabic fluently." Arabic-speaking customers flocked to his store to have their prescriptions filled. This was a first for Brooklyn and helped lead the way for other ethnic groups to enter the medical profession and, in particular, to speak the languages of many of their customers. During our teenage years, we got closer to Aunt Mary's children (Buddy and Dick); Aunt Rose B.'s children (Bobby, Ted, Jack, and Debbie who was named after Sitti Deeba); Uncle Alex and Aunt Jessie's children (Barbara, Mary Joan, and Georgie); Aunt Virginia and Uncle Al's children (Albert, Tommy, and Valerie). Dad and Mom got closer to all their nephews and nieces and often invited them to our house.

One incident that will always stand out in our family concerned Uncle Alex and Aunt Jessie's son, Georgie. One day we were visiting our Aunt Jessie on 9th Street in Brooklyn. They had a beautiful brownstone house. While we were eating in the dining room, we smelled some smoke. There was no Willie or Georgie in the dining room but there was smoke coming from under the bed! There was Willie and Georgie building a small bonfire beneath the bed. Did they get in trouble! Another incident involved Aunt Virginia's children. Mom liked to invite Aunt Virginia's children, Tommy and Valerie, to the house to play with Willie. Her older son, Albert, was "an angel" and never got into trouble but Willie, Tommy, and Valerie drove my mother and Aunt Virginia crazy. Well, whenever Valerie and Tommy visited, the next day Mom would have to call the plumber, the electrician, or others for repairs. Aunt Flo, who lived down the block, told of how she would watch the repairmen parade into the house. During one visit, Willie and Tommy stuck Valerie in the laundry shoot on the top floor. I don't know how she got pulled out, but she finally did. Mom didn't care. Valerie was safe and finally with her family.

George and I were focused on being the best students. Mom's biggest complaint about the two of us was that she would constantly tell us, "Put down your books and come downstairs and talk to me." She had the opposite with Willie. Willie didn't waste his time studying. He was always inquisitive and wanted to discover the world. He had fun and enjoyed growing up in Brooklyn with few worries—least of all schoolwork. Smart as a whip, he knew how to get out of schoolwork.

Academic students at our school were segregated from business and general education students. Girls were not encouraged to pursue a higher education. It was all right if a girl wanted to be a nurse or teacher. However, you were never encouraged to be a lawyer or doctor. I had outstanding grades in high school and college which would have helped me to get into law school or medical school. But there was one unspoken requirement for professional degrees: you must be a male.

In the 1950s, there were three types of diplomas – Academic, Commercial, and General. Boys and girls were found in all subject classes, in prefect (homeroom) classes and in the lunchroom.

The student population was so large that the four lunch periods not only included boys and girls, but started at 10:30 am and reached the size of over 600 students per lunch period. However, sport teams and physical education were different: girls and boys were segregated. Many years later, the New York City Board of Education changed the diplomas to Regents and Local. It wasn't until 2001 that Local diplomas ceased to exist. Physical education classes combined both girls and boys, and sports teams were regulated by the Federal Law (Title IV) to provide separate athletic teams for both sexes. The move to "raise standards" and to "eliminate separate but equal" was justification for the changes. I wonder if the Board of Education, currently called the Department of Education, may one day return to those three types of diplomas again. Time will tell. Isn't there a saying, "What goes around comes around?" George and I both earned Academic Diplomas and we were soon college bound. George went to Columbia University in the fall of 1956 and I attended New York University in the fall of 1957.

The years in Bay Ridge brought us closer to our families on both sides of the family. Aunt Rose's children (Bobby, Ted, Jack and Deborah) as well as Uncle Tom's children (Marcelle, Buddy, and Tommy) visited us quite often. Dad was so happy to see them. Dad also reunited with Uncle Galeb's children, Rose and Beddy G., and Alice (my namesake). Aunt Mary's children, Buddy and Dick, visited us from time to time. When Dad moved his ladies shop from Court Street in Manhattan to a large facility called Cury's Department Store in Ramsey, New Jersey, he got even closer to his sister Rose and nephews, Beddy G. and Buddy (Aunt Mary's son). Dad was absolutely thrilled to be around his family, but he missed his sister Jennie and brother Tom in Neon, Kentucky, as well as his brother Galeb in Paintsville, Kentucky. Rose G., Tony and the boys lived at 259 86th Street. We all spent a great deal of time with each other.

Giddi Cury had died in 1950 at the age of 72. His widow, "Aunt Adele," as we called her, was his second wife and my step-grandmother and godmother. She was the sister of the Metropolitan Archbishop Antony Bashir, head of the Syrian Orthodox Church in New York, and all North America. Aunt Adele lived with him at his official residence, 239 85th Street, just a few blocks away from us. She attended St. Mary's Church so I got to see her often. We met at the church on Sunday mornings, as well as during the week.

After the death of Archbishop Antony in 1966, Metropolitan Philip was elected and consecrated to replace him. One of the highlights of his early ministry was to drop the word "Syrian" from the official title of the archdiocese. From 1969, St. Mary's Syrian Orthodox Church was known as St. Mary's Antiochian Orthodox Church.

St. Mary's was built in 1951 and was the center for Antiochian Orthodoxy in Bay Ridge. It was remarkable that when I was growing up, my generation rarely associated with Catholics of the Eastern Rite Church in communion with Rome.

Strict, unwritten rules that you grew up with in those days meant that you socialized with those of the same nationality and religion. Today, this does not apply. But for first and second generation Lebanese and Syrian Americans, like my future husband and me, it did. Bay Ridge's population began to include many more ethnic groups such as Lebanese and Syrian first and second generation families. Little shops opened up serving all ethnic foods, especially Middle Eastern foods. At one time you had to go downtown to Atlantic Avenue in Brooklyn Heights to buy and eat our ethnic products and foods. Sahadi, Malko, and famous bakeries, such as the Damascus Bakery, permeated the popular Avenue and still do today. Now you can travel the local Bay Ridge streets, from the 60s through the 90s, and find Middle Eastern stores, restaurants, and bakeries such as Sally and George's Place, Karam Restaurant, and the MidEast Bakery.

Bay Ridge was, and still is, a special place to visit where restaurants and bakeries are lined up along Third, Fourth, and Fifth Avenues to entice the visitors and locals to eat food from Lebanon,

Syria, China, Poland, Italy, Greece, and Russia. International grocery stores are found along the avenues and are usually open seven days a week to serve visitors from all over the world. The famous Green Tea Room, the meeting place for decades, is no longer there but the popular ice cream parlor, called Hinsch's Confectionery (formerly called Flake's Confectionery in the 1920s and 1930s), located at 8518 5th Avenue, still serves the same food and delicious homemade ice creams and offers the same wonderful service to their customers. Yes, Dad had brought us home to mingle with our families and friends. Surely, Brooklyn was the "Center of the World," and Bay Ridge was, and still is, the cosmopolitan area in Brooklyn for all to visit and live in harmony.

Our family house at 157 83rd Street was a warm and welcoming home for family and friends to gather. When George graduated from high school, our parents invited the entire graduating class to the house. I found pictures of the party with a line written by Mom, "George deserved it." I also found a letter written by the principal of Fort Hamilton High School, Mr. Jon B. Leder, apologizing for not attending and stating, "May I, however, extend to you my sincere congratulations on the fine boy you have brought up and my best wishes for his future. I hope his party is as successful as he has been at Fort Hamilton." Yes, a little boy with third degree burns from the waist down, persevered, conquered his ailments and went on to graduate as head of his class. Although George had missed a year of schooling because of his accident, he still remained a top scholar and went on to Columbia University. Three degrees later, George earned a Doctoral Degree in Educational Administration from Rutgers State University.

I attended Washington Square College of Arts at New York University. I loved New York University and majoring in mathematics was one of my dreams. Since I was 8, I use to play school on the staircase with George and my friends. Teaching was a goal I yearned to achieve and teaching was what I was going to do. I made sure that I took the minimum twelve education credits and a major in pure mathematics to apply for a secondary school teaching job in the New York City Board of Education. Nothing was going to stop me from graduating and teaching. Nothing but a handsome and tall young man named Charlie (Syrian ancestry and Antiochian Orthodox—of course, thank you very much).

Chapter IV

My Charlie

After nearly three successful years at NYU from 1957 through 1959, I had just broken up with Teddy, my boyfriend of four years. I was devastated, to say the least. That was it! As I was crying in my bedroom, my mother walked in, sat at the side of my bed and tenderly placed her hand on my shoulder. "Alice," she said, "you always 'wear your heart on your sleeve'." Before you knew it, a 20-year-old woman was in the arms of her loving mother. She rocked me in her arms and compassionately offered pearls of wisdom. Mom was caring and loving to each of her children. *She favored none and loved all.* Her advice helped but I still had had it with boyfriends! What a waste of my time. It was New Year's Eve, 1959. Teddy seemed like a fading vision in my life. And this too was to pass, for it was only two months later that I met my future husband, Charlie.

It was the first weekend in February, 1960. Exams had finished at New York University and the spring semester had begun. I decided to go out with my girlfriends to see the movie *Bramble Bush* at the Dyker Theatre on 86th Street in Bay Ridge. My girlfriends and I met at the home of Vivian Farkouh, Charlie's sister. The Farkouh family lived in a two-family house at 458 85th Street. Vivian was a year younger than I and had graduated from

Fort Hamilton High School in 1958. Since her home was not too far from the Dyker Theatre, we decided to walk over to Vivian's house, pick her up and go to the next show. But just as Vivian was getting ready to go with us, she had an accident in her bedroom. She spilled almost the entire bottle of Shalimar—a very expensive French perfume—all over her dresser. Her brother, Charlie, a New York City Transit Patrolman, had just finished showering and was seated at the kitchen table, clad only in a white, terry cloth bathrobe. All my girlfriends hovered over him and began to flirt with him. This six-foot hulk of a man looked like an Adonis to me. He was unbelievably handsome. His dark and curly black hair was still wet, his heavy beard was dark since he had not shaved in over 24 hours, and his long and curly black eyelashes extended at least two inches over his green eyes. He had finished his midnight to eight tour of duty from the night before and was just getting ready for another tour of duty that evening. Nevertheless, I wasn't going to join the group and make a fool of myself! I had better things to do. One infatuation that ended in a disaster was enough for me. Besides, I was sure that he was not wearing anything under that robe. I didn't have any proof, but I just knew it! Why did my girlfriends give him the time of day? Well, maybe because he appeared charming, looked handsome, and was available! Perhaps he was flirting with them as well.

I rushed into the bedroom to help Vivian and to get away from Charlie and my girlfriends who were obviously flirting with him. Not me. Remember, I was through with boys. I had my career ahead of me. Vivian and I dabbed ourselves all over with the sweet-smelling French perfume. Did we smell! Nicely, but still overly saturated with perfume. After we cleaned up all the expensive French perfume, we decided we were ready to leave for the movies. Charlie wasn't even in my mind. Well, *I* found out later that Vivian's brother wanted to know "who the girl was that refused to sit in the kitchen" with him. That was how I got my first date with Charlie.

My grandmother, Sitti Nellie, in front of our
family house at 157 83rd Street in Bay Ridge,
Brooklyn. *(1957)*

I will never forget the following months. I had begun my new
classes for the spring semester and was engrossed in my college
work at NYU. It was my junior year and I was getting ready to
complete my B.A. degree in Mathematics. I was in my study
working on a project when Charlie called. He wanted to go on a
date . . . . Only a movie and out for a bite to eat. He picked me up
on a weekday evening. Sitti Nellie was in the kitchen with Mom
when the doorbell rang. It was Charlie. I ran to the door and was
so happy to see this attractive off-duty policeman dressed in a
blue suit, white shirt and matching tie entering the foyer. When I
was getting my coat to leave, I didn't realize that Sitti Nellie entered the living room. She had Parkinson's disease and spoke in
"broken English." I was relieved to see that Charlie did not understand a word she said, but I did. In broken English, she told

An official departmental portrait of Charlie
(Charles) Farkouh, my handsome New
York City Transit Police Officer. *(1954)*

him, "My Alice, she a no leave her books during the school week
to go on a date. This a means she is goin marry you." Oh! What a
way to chase your first date away or to assure you that you
wouldn't get a second date. I was so embarrassed! Charlie quietly
took me to the side so as not to embarrass my grandmother and
asked, "What did she say?" Thank God for that! I told him that it
wasn't important and swiftly moved him out of the house so Sitti
Nellie would not ask any more personal questions. Oh, but was-
n't she a wise owl. She must have seen something in my eyes
when Charlie entered the house for the first time. The next few
weeks were wonderful and I knew from the moment Charlie entered the front door on that first date that my grandmother was
right. I was going to marry that handsome cop one day, and very
soon. Sitti Nellie was right on the button!

Charlie was not his real name. It was "Shukri" but he didn't
like that name and was known as Charlie since he was a child. His

Charlie and me at our official engagement party. *(May 15, 1960)*

childhood friends on the block had nicknamed him Charlie and that was the end of the name Shukri. Well, Dad wanted me to marry a Syrian Orthodox Christian. Charlie was not only of Syrian ancestry but his religious background was Syrian Orthodox. Bingo! Charlie was just what the doctor ordered—I mean what "Dad" ordered. Oh, who cared. It was what *I* ordered. He was "my Charlie." We had a wonderful courtship. We met in February, got engaged in May, and married in September. It was like a whirlwind entered my life. During the period from our engagement until September 18 when we got married, we were busy bees. We shopped for an apartment, enjoyed the summer, and just had fun. I will never forget my Dad's disbelief at how fast it all happened. Dad was very happy with my choice, but he still had to check Charlie out. Who was this police officer who had swept his only daughter off her feet? He was going to find out and quick. Oh, by the way, when we got engaged, I still had to be home by 10 p.m. That was impossible since Charlie finished his summer tour at 10 p.m. and the night was young. When my father would ask me the following day if I was home by 10 p.m., I would "Yes, Dad" to death. Mom covered for me, and we left it like that. Mom never questioned me. Only Dad. Mom told him not to worry because I would not break any of his rules.

Uncle Alex knew Charlie's family very well. So, when he found out that his niece was dating Shukri Farkouh's son, he told Dad right away about Charlie's wonderful and respected family. Dad checked out his bank account as well. Not just anyone was going to marry his daughter. The only thing Dad was upset about was the fact that very few Lebanese and Syrian men had a career as a law enforcement officer. They didn't make a lot of money. His daughter was supposed to marry someone of wealth. Oh well, his little girl had wrapped her father around her little finger. He couldn't object and make her unhappy. Not Dad.

As is the custom in our family, Charlie had to ask for my hand in marriage. Dad was informed by the peacemaker (my mother) that he was going to be asked in early May. In fact, Mom told Dad and the next evening it was planned for Charlie to break the question to his future father-in-law. Dad arrived home from work by 10 p.m. His business was located in Ramsey, New Jersey and it was an hour's ride to Bay Ridge. Charlie started to talk to Dad for over an hour. He talked about everything under the sun but what he was supposed to ask Dad. It was now 11:30 p.m. and Dad had to get up early the next morning. In a very subtle manner, Dad lit a wooden match and put it up to the glass crystal of his watch and sheepishly said, "Well, it is very late and I think I have to turn in now." Well, I thought I was going to die of embarrassment. What was wrong with Charlie? By this time, Charlie was perspiring and he knew that this was his last opportunity to speak up. He quickly asked Dad for my hand in marriage. Dad smiled, chuckled a little, and responded, "Our family will be very happy to have you marry Alice." Dad quickly left Charlie and me and went to bed. I walked Charlie to the car since it was past the bewitching hour. I figured he was ready to go home. But he wasn't. He opened up the glove compartment of the car and pulled out a small, grey velvet box. I still have the box. I only visited a jewelry store with Charlie once to select the ring setting, a tiffany mount. That was it. Charlie opened the ring box and to my surprise, a sparkling old-fashioned cut diamond ring in a tiffany setting peered out of the box. He then held me in his strong arms and proposed. When I accepted, he put the ring on my finger. We had a very long goodnight kiss before he left. I ran up the stairs to my parents' bedroom. As usual, Mom was reading a story in *Reader's Digest* and Dad was reading the *Daily News*. I showed him the ring. He mumbled," Good thing it's a big stone . . . . mmm . . . . he has good taste." It is customary in a Syrian marriage that your husband's love is reflected in the size of the diamond. Well, Charlie made a very good decision if he was going to get Bill Cury's daughter. The night before we were to be wed, Dad told me that if I changed my mind, I could always come back. That wasn't going to happen. I loved Charlie.

To Charlie, I was the "apple of his eye." I got this nickname from Charlie. Every Saturday night during the summer which lasted from May 18 until our wedding day on September 18, Charlie would purchase a candy apple from Philip, a candy vendor, at the Stillwell Avenue train station in Coney Island. At the end of his midnight tour, he would deposit it outside my front door. The first time he dropped it off, he attached a note ripped out of the *Daily News* that had the following scribbled on it, "This apple is for the apple of my eye. Chas." I still have that piece of paper. To my surprise, Philip moved to Staten Island and opened a candy store on Barrett Avenue off Victory Boulevard. Charlie and I visit him from time to time and reminisce about Stillwell Avenue in Coney Island. Isn't it a small world?

We got married on a beautiful and sunny Sunday afternoon on September 18, 1960. It was difficult to change Charlie's vacation time. President Nikita Khrushchev of Russia had planned a visit to the United Nations on October 12, 1960. Since the New York City Police, as well as the New York City Transit Police, were on overtime to secure the city, there was no way to adjust vacation schedules. I was busy studying for finals in May, so Charlie and Mom planned almost the entire wedding. When it

Our wedding day at the Hotel Bossertt in downtown
Brooklyn, New York. *(September 18, 1960)*

came to grades, I was not happy to just pass. If it wasn't an "A," it wasn't good enough for me. Summer came and went. We were married in September at St. Mary's Syrian Orthodox Church. Although we only had a little over 100 guests at the wedding reception, we had almost 500 guests attend the wedding ceremony. That was unbelievable!

Charlie and I rented a one-bedroom apartment at 247 Bay 17th Street in Bensonhurst, Brooklyn. It was small and I wasn't used to living in an apartment house after living with my parents in a large five-bedroom Tudor house in Bay Ridge. We now lived about ten minutes away from Bay Ridge. I missed my parents, but knew I had to cut the apron strings. George and Willie missed me as well. I will never forget how George, who was one of our ushers, cried like a baby at the ceremony. At the wedding reception, Willie came up to me and reminded me "that you will always be a Cury." He was a junior usher and looked so handsome. He meant what he said and quickly turned on his heels and walked away. He had proudly given me his message. Since we got married at the beginning of the fall semester, I had to miss a semester of school. Dad was very upset to see that I was going to miss attending college that fall term, but I promised him that I would graduate. He knew that I always kept a promise.

However, little did I know that Charlie was not going to be able to fund my college tuition like my father had done. He was a NYC Transit Patrolman and couldn't afford the $40 a credit at NYU. His Patrolman's salary of $4,500 a year could not sustain such a high tuition. It hurt me when he told me that I would have to go to Brooklyn College and could not graduate from NYU unless I asked for scholarship money. I cried for a week. Finally, I had to either pay my tuition or transfer. I was indeed surprised when the financial officer approved funds to pay for almost my entire last year's tuition at NYU. When I got the news, Charlie said, "They didn't want to lose one of their top students." I had to promise the financial officer that I was going to enter the field of education. Little did he know that I was three months pregnant with our first child, Cathy! I attended the first half of my senior term pregnant. I still went by my maiden name, Alice Barbara Cury. Charlie was furious. However, I told him that I may receive some awards and if I used my married name, the professors would not recognize that it was Alice Cury. Reluctantly, Charlie gave in but he still was not a happy camper.

When I was elected into the Phi Beta Kappa Society in the spring of my senior year, I decided to wear a maternity dress for the first time underneath my ceremonial robes. When I removed the robes during the reception, I shocked my professors. It was very hard camouflaging a pregnancy to attend different schools in the city for my observation course. I knew I couldn't take a student teaching class, because there was no way I could completely fool everyone. I couldn't be a student teacher because, at that time, under no circumstances could you work for the New York City Board of Education while pregnant. I was grateful to have a wonderful Observation teacher at NYU who taught me the key elements of how to observe, write and execute an effective lesson. Her teachings were the foundation for my teaching skills as a newly appointed teacher. She took us to private, parochial, and public schools. We would observe and return to her class to discuss our experiences.

Life in Bensonhurst was interesting. I can still remember the bakery around the corner from Bay 17th Street. The freshly baked rye bread filled the air with an aroma that I will never forget. It was not uncommon for me to run around the corner to Cropsey Avenue and buy a loaf of bread. The owner would slice it for me and I would rush back home and prepare breakfast for Charlie's return from a midnight to eight tour of duty. I fussed over him. I even pressed his underwear for the first three months of mar-riage—that is, until I got pregnant. I had terrible morning sick-ness. Well, that was the last time his underwear got pressed.

Riis Park was not too far away. My friends and relatives would meet us at the beach on the weekend for a grand time. Mom and Dad would come, as well as Aunt Flo and Uncle Alex, to spend the entire day at the beach. Mom would fry the eggplant and squash and prepare sandwiches made out of Syrian bread. Yes, Syrian bread. Not pita bread as it is commonly called now. Aunt Flo would make the most delicious Italian peppers and veal sandwiches. Aunt Jessie and Uncle Alex would come down from their brownstone home on Ninth Street in Brooklyn with freshly baked Ebinger cakes and buns . . . .mmm . . . . especially the crumb cake and the seven-layer cake. What wonderful memories we have from those days at Riis Park in the summer of 1961. Of course, I was in my eighth and ninth months of pregnancy and was too uncomfortable to enjoy the cool salt water, but it was nice and cool at the beach. Air conditioners were just becoming rea-sonable to buy if your landlord had the right voltage; our

Charlie and me, at left, sunbathing with friends on the beach at Riis Park, Brooklyn. *(August 7, 1961)* I was expecting our first child, Catherine Marie.

apartment house was not ready for air conditioners. So, I suffered from heat exhaustion during that hot summer.

It was the night of September 3, 1961. The next day would be Labor Day. Charlie had warned me for over a month that I could give birth any day *but Labor Day*. The Belt Parkway was packed on Labor Day and traffic would be a disaster. Well, I told him that I wasn't due until September 9. Our first child, Catherine Marie, wouldn't hear of it. On September 3, the night before Labor Day, my labor pains began. Charlie had to rush me to the hospital before midnight. Charlie and I arrived at Beth El Hospital a little too soon. Dr. Sisskind, the resident doctor, told my husband and me to take a long walk around Beth El Hospital. As we were walking, I heard patients crying out from one area of the building. "Gee, Charlie, there must have been a bus accident." Charlie just smiled. Two hours later, I joined the screaming voices in the maternity wing. This showed you how much we knew about pregnancy, giving birth, etc. How naïve I was in the early 1960s. Was that good or bad? Perhaps after looking back and knowing how

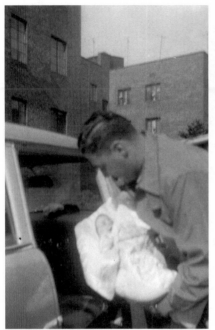

Proud father, Charlie, taking our first newborn, Catherine Marie, from the car outside our Bensonhurst apartment. *(September 7, 1961)*

Proud mother, me, with baby, Cathy, heading towards our apartment house. *(September 7, 1961)*

medicine has progressed, I would agree that the mother and child are safer today with the advances in medicine.

Cathy was born the next day at 5:30 a.m. on September 4, 1961—Labor Day! What a beautiful baby girl. She had blue eyes, needed a hair cut, and skin so pale and pink. A small crop of blonde hair peeked out from her shining black curly hair. The nurses in the maternity wing enjoyed combing her hair and donning her in a pink ribbon and pink gown. Charlie and I named her after our mothers, Catherine Marie Farkouh, although we changed the spelling of her first name so that she would have the same initial as her father, Charlie. I enjoyed the next few months taking care of her. She was my baby doll. She was the sister I never had. There were two things I enjoyed doing as a child—playing mommy and playing school. First came being a real mommy, not a pretend mommy. Next was the promise to my Dad. I promised that I would get my degree so I decided to return in the spring of 1962 to NYU to complete the last half of my senior year while Charlie's mom, Marie, and Charlie took care of baby Cathy.

My father was getting exhausted driving back and forth to work from northern New Jersey to Bay Ridge. My parents asked my permission to move to Ramsey, New Jersey, the town where Dad had his business. They didn't want to leave me and the baby but it was the right thing for Dad. Dad and Mom sold their house in Bay Ridge and moved to 5 Lakeview

My graduation portrait from New York University. *(1962)*

Terrace in Ramsey, New Jersey, a couple of minutes from Dad's department store on Route 17 North.

I graduated from NYU in May of 1962 with a Bachelor of Arts Degree (cum laude) in Mathematics. Cathy attended the graduation as well. However, my mother, mother-in-law and Cathy couldn't watch the ceremony since there were no such things as disposable diapers and someone didn't pin the diaper correctly on Cathy! Need I say more?

I had been elected into the Phi Beta Kappa Society, achieved cum laude status, was on the Dean's List, and was the recipient of the Woodrow Wilson Award. I was very determined to show Dad and Mom that I had kept my promise and graduated. Now, I had to keep a promise to my husband about having more children, as well as a promise to the NYU financial advisor about becoming a teacher if he gave me scholarship money to complete my last semester, and a promise to myself that I was going to be a teacher one day. I had made up my mind that I was going to

77

return to Fort Hamilton High School as a mathematics teacher one day, one day . . . .

Well, I had three promises to keep. After Cathy, a handsome baby boy named Charles was born on March 28, 1963. Charles was born with the most beautiful blue eyes and, like his Daddy, had a crop of hair. Both Cathy and Charles kept their blue eyes. My Dad was so happy to see that finally his grandchildren would have his blue eyes. Charles had round shoulders and a great appetite. He always looked serious and observed and remembered everything. A little over two years went by and Charles was followed by our second handsome baby boy, Stephen, who was born on May 8, 1965. Although Stephen came three weeks early and was the smallest of the three babies, he ultimately grew to be six feet, and the tallest. Stephen had blue eyes as well, but they turned hazel, the color of his Mom and Dad's eyes. He had the shoulders of a football player and he was forever laughing and smiling. I always said he was the baby "born with a smile." The children were God's gift to Charlie and me in the first four years of marriage.

Right after Charles was born, our landlord raised the rent five dollars a month. That was it. Charlie was not going to pay a penny more for a one-bedroom apartment. Charlie packed us up and we moved to Staten Island and purchased a new duplex at 53 Jefferson Ave. in Dongan Hills. The Verrazano-Narrows Bridge was not built yet so we had to use the 69th Street ferryboat to go back and forth to Bay Ridge. It wasn't until the bridge was open for business on November 21, 1964 that the 69th Street ferryboat was terminated forever. With the coming of the bridge, it meant that our travel time back and forth to Brooklyn would be less than 20 minutes. That was great!

The first six years of marriage were fun. I enjoyed raising the children, going to P.T.A. meetings and doing fun things with the family. However, I was sad to know that I hadn't become a schoolteacher. Couldn't I continue to be a good mother and wife and start a career as well? We could sure use the money since police officers were not paid well. I had been tutoring mathematics from time to time. I even went as far as to take a NYU sunrise morning class at 6 a.m. in physics while feeding my third child, Stephen. I earned an A–. It is amazing that young girls like me were never encouraged to take more than the minimum classes in science and mathematics. That wasn't true for me in mathematics, but I had always regretted not taking physics. I had earned a 100 on the Chemistry Regents, but I was never encouraged to take much science in high school. Well, now I not only took more science in college, but I went the extra mile and took college physics at sunset with Stephen in my arms.

When Stephen was two and a half years old, I found out that The City University of New York offered a free master's degree to a full-time or part-time teacher who taught in the New York City Public Schools. What a deal! Charlie agreed, but only on the condition that we would have three more children one day. I had taken and passed a substitute mathematics examination for New York City in April of 1967. One last step in the process to become a teacher was to get my father's permission to teach. Yes, I needed his permission. That was the proper thing to do in a Lebanese and Syrian home. Of course, Dad was thrilled. Charlie wasn't. He couldn't believe that a married woman with three children had to ask for her father's permission to go to work. That was the custom of Lebanese and Syrians in those days. Parents would always be given respect no matter how old the children were. Things have changed now.

I was ready. However, to my dismay in September of 1967, the United Federation of Teachers (UFT) went on strike. My children were attending P.S. 11 in Staten Island. So I decided to be a "scab" and teach fifth grade at P.S. 11 during the strike. I worked for 12 days and had a ball. I loved teaching the eager faces of fifth graders. Did I make a mistake and follow my heart as a secondary schoolteacher in mathematics? Three decades later I figured it out. It was not the love of teaching fifth graders or ninth through twelfth graders; it was the love of teaching and seeing students learn. After the strike ended, I decided to register for the spring term at Richmond College, an upper school division of the City University in Staten Island. I could go to classes in the late afternoons and evenings while Charlie or Nora, my middle-aged Italian neighbor, watched the children. The only drawback was that I had to pay Nora $25.00 per day. I also had the opportunity to teach mathematics in an independent school on the Island for $25.00 per day. If I accepted the private school position, then I would not be making any money after paying the baby sitter. The private school would pay me $25.00 per day; the public school would give me $40.00 per day. So I chose to go the public school route. Would I have changed my mind if I knew what the school for the privileged was all about? You answer that question! I already know the response.

While I was waiting on line registering for classes at Richmond College's bursar's office, I met my first professional friend, Terry Burke. She informed me that a substitute mathematics teacher was needed at Port Richmond High School. The teacher had to take an immediate maternity leave. She had no rights. Pregnant and out! I decided to visit the school where I met Isaac (Ike) Feinberg, one of the most influential educators in my teaching career. At that time, Ike's title was Chairman of the Mathematics Department. This would soon change to the title of Assistant Principal of Supervision with the advent of women's rights and the fact that instruction was on the same pay scale as administration and supervision. He was so pleased to see my credentials and informed me that I could start the next day. I was assigned classes in algebra and geometry. I rushed home and promised Charlie that I would only teach until the permanent teacher returned in February. Then we would begin to have our fourth child, a promise that I never kept and one that Charlie will remind me of until my dying day.

To the sorrow of our family, Dad died of a massive heart attack in August, 1968. He was only 59 years old. My younger brother was almost 21 and Mom was 54. The two decided to take over Cury's Department Store. Willie's name was changed to Bill by Mom. He was now her Bill. Bill was innovative and creative. We always knew that. He was able to extend the store to include skis and other sport items. They did so well that Mom and Bill decided to stop renting and bought their own property. They built a large sport shop very close to their old one. Cury's Sport Shop opened its doors in July of 1978. Sport enthusiasts came from all areas of New Jersey, New York, and near the border of Canada. Their business thrived. Cury's Sport Shop soon was renowned for the quality of its merchandise, the expertise of the salespersons, and the family touch to its business. It achieved an award for being one of the best sports stores along the East Coast. Today, it is still run by family: Bill, Linda, and their two sons, William Beddy Cury III and Christopher. Linda's mentor was Mom. She learned to be an excellent buyer, saleswoman, and business entrepreneur. She has always been special to me. I am so proud of them both and know if Dad and Mom were alive they would say the same thing. Their store mottos, "Hurry to Curys" and "Think Snow," are two that will always stand out in my mind. Yes, Cury's Sport Shop is a place of business for family and enthusiasts of winter, spring, and summer sports.

As I moved through my career, I always remember that Dad gave us a choice of working with him or going to college. That was the beauty of having wonderful parents who were oriented towards family. They gave us choices. Bill chose to become a businessman. George and I chose to become teachers and administrators. George continued his career as a science teacher, principal, and administrator earning his Doctorate in Educational Administration from Rutgers University. He had a daughter, Tracey, early in life. However, circumstances separated him from Tracey until 1990 when he reunited with her. Unfortunately, George died suddenly in February of 1995. Tracey married a wonderful young man, Mark. They were blessed with three beautiful children. She and her family have become close with me and I am known as their "Aunt Alice." We all became successful in our careers. Why?

Our parents gave us choices. That's what it's all about. Build your family on a sound foundation and allow them to choose.

I can't leave Charlie out. If it wasn't for Charlie, not only would we not have such a wonderful family, but I wouldn't have been able to pursue my goal to become an educator. Yes, Charlie is the kind of husband who gives and never asks anything in return. Except for three more children!

Chapter V

A Dream Come True

It was my first day at Port Richmond High School. The school was located in Mariners Harbor, which was a blue collar neighborhood of "old Staten Islanders" whose ancestors go back to the original settlers of the Island. The minority families were predominantly black. We lived on the South Shore which was predominantly Italian and Irish with almost no families of color. When we came to Staten Island in August 1963 our son, Charles, was only five months old. My husband had bought a brand new duplex home in Dongan Hills. All our savings were spent on bedroom furniture for Cathy and baby Charlie. Our neighbors, who shared the adjoining duplex, were Jerry and Helen McMahon. At that time, they had five girls. After Stephen was born, I remember Helen looking at Stephen in the bassinet and proudly telling me that she was pregnant again. Marion was born eight months later and became Stephen's closest friend. In fact, Stephen and Marion were inseparable. They even went as far as to share their gum—one chew for me, one chew for you, and so on. It was a miracle that when Stephen got the chicken pox, Marion didn't.

One day, many years later, Jerry plucked up the courage to come over and ask Charlie something that had apparently been bothering him for a long time. "How come the neighbors on the

My career in education began here at Port Richmond High School, Staten Island. *(Photo courtesy Port Richmond High School Yearbook, Soundings, 1969)*

other side of us were so friendly when you moved in but when we moved into the duplex a few months before you, they didn't give me or my family the time of day?" So, Charlie decided one evening to go over and find out. He rather gingerly put that question directly to our neighbor. "How come when my family and I moved into the neighborhood, you and your wife heated up the baby bottle and brought food over, but when Jerry moved in with his wife and five girls, you didn't do anything for them?" He replied, "Because you're one of us." "What do you mean?" Charlie asked. "Because you are Italian." "No, I'm not. I'm not Italian," Charlie responded. Now, it was our neighbor's turn to ask, "What are you then?" "We're Syrian," Charlie said. Our neighbor then came out with a statement that Charlie will never forget. "Sicilians are okay too."

I remember another time when our son, Charles, brought home a boy from the neighborhood to play, our neighbor commented to me, "I see that Charles has a new friend." I didn't get the gist of his remark until a few days later when Charles brought the same school friend home again. Then I figured it out. His

My first faculty yearbook photo.
(Photo courtesy Port Richmond High School Yearbook, Soundings, 1969)

friend was black. Was our neighbor implying that it wasn't acceptable for our son to play with the boy next door to him because he was black? If so, that was his hang-up, not ours. Well, Charles continued to select his own friends, regardless of race or color but sad to say, at that time prejudice permeated Staten Island's South Shore where we lived.

It was different on the North Shore. For example, when my neighbors found out that I was going to work in Mariners Harbor, they were very upset. They couldn't understand why I would want to teach in a "black school." Of course, students from black and white families attended the school. So why then was it labeled "a black school"? There was a lot of prejudice and intolerance then. These traits were unacceptable to my family even though I was born in Kentucky where there was not one family who was Catholic, Jewish, or black in our town. A black lady was allowed to come into the town and help our mother with George and me, but she always had to leave at dusk. I loved her dearly. So did the rest of the family. Mom reminded me later in life that, as a little girl, I had once asked our housekeeper, "Is you black for being black or is you black from drinking cossie (coffee)." Mom said that the lady turned to me, hugged me real tight and replied, "Alice, that's the sweetest thing anyone ever asked me." I grew up with prejudice all around me in the South until I was a teenager and I wasn't going to hear it anymore. I replied to my friends and neighbors that they had their personal beliefs but I wasn't going along with them. To me, Port Richmond High School was a beautiful place to start my teaching career and I was ready.

It was November 3, 1967: my first teaching day at Port Richmond High. I taught the first two classes and then proceeded to

Mr. Isaac Feinberg
Math Department Chairman

Mrs. Miriam Zucker

Two great teachers, two great "mentors." Ike and Miriam's advice and wisdom helped guide me through my early days at Port Richmond High School. They were my "teachers"! *(Photo courtesy Port Richmond High School Yearbook, Soundings, 1969)*

the stockroom where I ordered my chalk, erasers, paper clips, markers, grade book, note paper, late passes, and composition paper. The stockman took my order and then made a call. In a couple of minutes, Ike Feinberg, the Chairman of the Mathematics Department, entered the stockroom and politely said, "Alice, I would like to observe you first before you take the job." I looked at him a little puzzled. I was 27, graduated cum laude from NYU, had three children ranging from 2 ½ to 6 years old, managed a three-bedroom house, cooked, sewed, and was (I hope) a loving wife. "Alright," I replied. Ike came into the class later in the day and observed me teaching first-term geometry. He wrote on my observation report the following: "The boys and girls in this class are indeed fortunate that you came to their rescue, after their chaotic introduction to this term. Your enthusiasm, interest and vitality are contagious. As you gain in experience, these qualities and your knowledge of mathematics will undoubtedly combine to make you an outstanding teacher. Good luck! —Isaac W. Feinberg, Chairman."

I will never forget what he told me at the post conference. At the time, I was not nervous when he observed me but I soon learned to be uptight whenever he came in for he was not only an outstanding teacher, but he was a perfectionist. He had set his standards high and expected others to do the same. That is probably why I am the teacher I am today. I have set my standards high as well. Maybe I am not always perfect, but my goals are like Ike's. That is why I admire a person like Ike Feinberg for what he has done for me, and for his other teachers and students as well. I salute him and will always use him as an example to my teachers and students. Ike cleared his throat and told me that I had an "innate ability for teaching" and that he was very happy to have me join the Mathematics Department for the remaining term. I was a Mathematics Major at NYU so I had an excellent background in my subject area. I knew I could do the job and do it well. As one of my colleagues said, "To educate, you have to be educated." I knew that Ike would be happy to have me. I also knew that I would love teaching mathematics from the first day I was in the classroom. My Chairman Ike was also a great help, especially when I needed help with audiovisual aides, motivating lessons, or just talking to him when I felt a lesson didn't go well.

One of my dearest friends in the Mathematics Department at Port Richmond was my mentor, Miriam Zucker. Although she was not my official "mentor," I made her one. I found myself sharing lunches with her, working together during our common prep period and arriving purposely ten minutes early for my class so I could stand outside her door to watch her teach. She was my idol, my friend, my role model. I learned how to perfect my lessons, to make use of my Delaney cards in a way that could also give me an immediate glance of data when I needed it, and to motivate lessons. Delaney cards were developed for teachers to take student attendance by classroom seat location. Miriam finally invited me into her class to observe her when she noticed me "eavesdropping" every day outside her door. I adored her. I was an American of Lebanese and Syrian background and Ike

Photo from the early 1970's of myself (at left by blackboard) with student staff of the PRHS mathematics magazine, *Zenith*.
(Photo courtesy Port Richmond High School)

and Miriam were Jewish. There was no closer bond than among the three of us, not only on a personal basis, but also on a professional basis as well. We socialized with each other outside of school, attended yearly professional weekends in the Catskills, and attended special functions together.

Could someone ever burst my "bubble of enthusiasm" for teaching? It almost happened.

I will never forget the time that a parent arrived at my door during the second year of my career and demanded to speak to me about why I made her daughter get a late pass. Screaming at the top of her lungs so my students could hear, she shouted, "You have no right to do this since my daughter comes all the way from Manhattan to this forsaken school. I'll have the Chancellor take your license away from you." After class, I went into the mathematics office and started to cry. Ike loaned me his clean, white, folded handkerchief and told me "not to worry" because I was "following school policy." Instead, he was upset to know that a parent was allowed to find me in the classroom.

After I finished school, I told Charlie what had happened. As usual, whenever I had a problem, Charlie had a wonderful and calming solution. He reminded me of my promise and said that I should quit now and we could have that fourth child. I thought about it and searched my heart. Why should the other students in my classes be deprived of my teaching and love for them? They needed a capable and effective teacher and I was not going to give in to an irate parent. I will never forget that incident for it had made me become a better teacher. I later found out that the mother was having marital problems and was upset that her child was having conflicts in traveling to a school so far away from her home. Ike's handkerchief remained with me for over three decades. I was too embarrassed to hand it back to him. Instead, I found that whenever I had a problem at school, I would go to the bottom drawer of my dresser at home and there, hidden under my gloves and evening bags, was Ike's handkerchief to remind me of who I was, where I had been, and where I was going. "Never say you can't, never say you can't…"

My friend and colleague, Miriam, died of cancer five years into my career. I took over as the faculty adviser for *Zenith*, Port Richmond High School's mathematics magazine. Miriam's husband was a dear friend of ours and he decided to give me Miriam's library of mathematics books. I have always cherished her books and shared them with my students over the decades. Many articles and reports have been written by students using these reference books. When I needed to find motivations, such as the "rope stretchers of Egypt," a mathematics poem, or learn about how the Greeks used the properties of the parabola and the sun's rays to burn the wooden ships of their enemies, I would consult Miriam's book collection. I also use to tell my students about a mathematics "trick" that Miriam showed me to help students remember some mathematical concepts. I can still see her warm smile, hear her advice about teaching, and read her notes along the margins of her books. *Thank you, Miriam.*

At Port Richmond High School, I built many long-lasting friendships with students who later became teachers, nurses, and doctors. Other endearing friendships continued with school secretaries like Grace, Claire, Rose, and Betty; teachers like Miriam, Phyllis, Johanna, Joan, Kathy, Irene, John, Peaches, Bob, Jack, Tony, Harvey, Dr. John Palumbo, and Paul; assistant principals like Ike, Walter, John, Beverly, and Nick; and finally, an outstanding principal and—later on—colleague and mentor, like Herbert Balish. How did Herbert Balish come into my professional life? Well, it started with the racial tensions which exploded at Port Richmond High School in the late 1960s.

In one infamous incident, trouble started in the school's cafeteria and quickly spread throughout the building, from the first floor up to the third. White students hid under desks, a Black Panther flag waved in the cafeteria, and teachers and students, both black and white, were scared out of their wits. The year was 1970 and the Black Panther movement was strong. Port Richmond High had suffered from a lack of strong leadership and the inability to cope with the Civil Rights Movement that began a few years before. A racial riot broke out in the school. I remember running up to the third floor and seeing one of my students huddled under a student desk shivering with fright. I yelled out to him, "What's wrong?" I noticed broken glass scattered along the floor adjacent to the windows. The sun streamed through the smashed frames, inundating the classrooms with a blinding white light and the explosive sounds of turmoil from down below in the cafeteria. He wouldn't come out of his "shelter." This 16-year-old young man, six feet in stature, shivered with fright, tears rolling down his face in a steady stream. He responded, "Mrs. Farkouh, *I can't*. I'm afraid. I want to go home. Help me. The black students are running around with sticks and broken glass. Help me . . . . I have to go home . . . . have to go home, *I can't* stay here." He cried. "Never say you can't...Never say you can't." He had triggered memories from my own past.

As I looked outside the hallway, I could see three black students shouting and cursing . . . . freedom, freedom, we will overcome. In my sight was a young black man whom I had befriended, and who was one of my current math students. I came up to him and said, "What's wrong?" No response from him. A chill pierced my heart and a terrible fear suddenly ran down my spine like a shower of icy water on a cold winter's night. I will never forget how the kind and respectful student I knew had now changed his demeanor. He was no longer smiling and pleasant. What had happened to him? What had triggered this instant "transformation?" Or was it instant? Had it been bottling up inside of him for a long time? I later realized that it wasn't an instant transformation, but centuries of prejudice and hatred manifested by our race, our lily-white race. Our school had never addressed the issue of racial problems, nor had the school system and, as a result, we had wild students; black and white students fighting, cursing or hiding in obscurity behind their façade of peace and tranquility.

My memories of growing up in the South during the years prior to the Civil Rights Movement were still very vivid. I had witnessed the boys' and girls' bathrooms labeled "Colored Boys" and "Colored Girls." I remembered the odor on the buses, and my parents discussing the problem that city officials had made it a point not to clean the back of the bus where the local "coloreds" were forced to sit. Only the front of the bus, where the white passengers sat, was ever scrubbed down. Flashbacks came to me in those chaotic minutes as I also remembered the unkind words one of my uncles had once for blacks. Yet, I also remembered the black woman who helped my mother to raise me in my early years, as one of the most caring, loving persons to have entered my life. I remembered how tender and kind my Mom had been to her helper and to other blacks. My brothers and I grew up in an environment of love and harmony, and so we felt the constant need to defend a people that were not welcomed as our equals in the 1940s and 1950s in the South. I only think of this period of time because I remembered the deep-seated racism. Prejudice was overt in the South, but that was not so much the case in the North. Prejudice in the North and, in particular, in New York City public schools, such as Port Richmond High School, was subtle but, during this racial riot, it was as if all the hell of past decades had broken loose. It was white students fighting black students. Not all of them were involved but enough to cause a panic. It was white students who were not involved in the arguments who hid under desks, afraid to move; it was our school under siege. We needed a leader and quickly. We needed a "knight in white armor" to come and rescue our school. Our next principal arrived, but not in white armor.

Chapter VI

Arrival of the Knight in White Armor

The knight in white armor didn't actually wear a sheet of metal but a suit, a crispy white shirt, and a new tie. I can't remember the color of his suit, but I will never forget his entrance into the school library at Port Richmond on a bright and beautiful March morning in 1971. The faculty was seated at tables anxiously awaiting the newly-appointed principal to speak to us. I remember who was sitting at my table: Peaches, one of my favorite physical education teachers; Kathy, the English teacher and my "forever" friend; Terry, the guidance counselor (who was responsible for my being hired); Johanna, one of the last German language teachers to be hired by the NYC Board of Education; and Joan, an extremely knowledgeable social studies teacher. I could see Bob, a physical education teacher, basketball coach, and "keeper of the student cafeteria," peering across the room as Herbert Balish entered. We were all anxious, wondering if our new principal could "solve the school's racial problems," something which his predecessors had failed to accomplish. I am sure that deep down we were all worried that perhaps he would fail; perhaps we would just continue to have another passing bureaucrat who would administer from top down.

Our "Knight in White Armor"—Herbert Balish. As
the new principal of Port Richmond High School in
1971, Mr. Balish set about restoring harmony and
academic pride to a school which had been
devastated by racial turmoil. *(Photo courtesy Port
Richmond High School Yearbook, Soundings, 1976)*

Mr. Balish entered the room with a smile that reminded me of
Lieutenant Columbo, the detective from the 1970's television se-
ries which was so popular back then. I can't remember if he had
the same stubby, unlit cigar as Columbo did, but when I think of
Herbert Balish now, I always remember that twinkle in his eye,
and the meticulous way he approached his work as he strived to
improve the city's school system.

Although Mom and Dad always taught me to evaluate a situation, use finesse, and think first before making a decision, I didn't
take their advice this time. As soon as Mr. Balish walked into the
library to meet the faculty, I knew he was going to be an asset to
the school. Mr. Balish was going to be the catalytic agent to
improve our school.

He was rather short in stature, had a full and robust face,
wore a smile across his face and spoke softly. He was fatherly and

charming. He greeted us, informed us that he was very fortunate to be appointed to Port Richmond High School and would be meeting each and every one of us in time. Many of the veteran teachers were doubtful. They felt that previously appointees had failed the school, and they hoped that history would not repeat itself. It didn't.

Herbert Balish would soon earn the reputation of being extremely bright, a promoter of excellence in teaching and learning, and firm but fair to students, as well as faculty. Parents admired him as well. When students did something wrong, he didn't usually suspend them. Instead, he matched the punishment with the "crime." If a student wrote graffiti on the walls, desks or the exterior of the building, they had to paint or clean up what they did. The rub was that it would have to be done on a Saturday, Sunday, or holiday. Who supervised the students? He did. I never spoke to any of the students who were caught, but evidently the number of suspensions, detentions, or special "jobs" slowly decreased as the terms passed. Did you want to spend your weekend cleaning up the area with the principal overseeing you? With a principal who chatted about your future aspirations, vocabulary, and your need to improve your schoolwork, you didn't want to be caught again. It was bad enough for five days but, on the weekend, *no way*! Seven days of education was not what they wanted. Rumors circulated that he also attended every sports game, indoor and outdoor, no matter what the weather was like. The school became his primary job; his personal life was secondary. Now that I look back, I can't recall his children or wife ever complaining about his devoting so much time to our school. In fact, it was not uncommon to be invited to his home for dinner after a special event at school. He *was* a special man. I soon grew to love my Mr. Balish. He was my ideal of a real leader. I hoped to become a principal one day and model myself after him. He was my special role model for life.

As Mr. Balish finished off his first school year at Port Richmond, he brought with him a serene and calming ambiance to the school. He *was* like Lieutenant Columbo on television! In his Socratic manner, he would never talk at you but would always pose questions about *why* and *how* or *what if*. He already knew the answers to his questions, but he wanted the responses to come from you. That was his style. The staff, students, and parents began to respect him. Faculty and staff soon realized that he meant business. That is, school business. As he quickly moved from floor to floor and class to class, you knew that the school was in good hands. It was not uncommon to find him in the teachers' cafeteria having his morning coffee and sharing his muffin with you. He would tell us that his wife, Faith, was making him watch his weight. That was his excuse for buying a freshly baked bran or corn muffin in the morning and sharing half of it with you as he discussed your opinion about an idea or problem. He would stroll around the student cafeteria as well, sit down with students and often join them at lunch. That's the way it was. Mr. Balish was quite respected by the superintendent and high school division administrators. He was placed on many committees, worked closely with parents and the community, and was indeed a friend to the United Federation of Teachers (the New York City Board of Education teachers union, commonly called the UFT). He respected teachers and usually complied with the UFT contract. When he broke a rule in the contract, you knew quite well that there was a good reason. Consequently, there were few teacher grievances.

One of the times he did not follow the contract actually involved me. As soon as he became the newly appointed principal, he decided to add a second college advisor position to the college office. The compensatory job (extra nonteaching jobs during a teacher's workday) was advertised and I decided to apply for it. I had just become a tenured mathematics teacher and was ready to provide extra service for the school. Mr. Balish interviewed me for almost an hour. I gave him my opinion about what I would do if I was selected as the second college advisor. I had just completed my first Master's Degree in Mathematics Education and was ready for the challenge. Since I had never had a compensatory job and was regularly appointed to the school, I was sure my appointment "was in the bag." You think? Not so.

Instead, Mr. Balish chose one of the school's regular substitute teachers who, in my opinion, was personable but not too strong academically. My bubble burst. My ego slipped into the drain. I went to the local chapter leader for the UFT to complain. He told me that I had the right to the job since I was qualified and had seniority over Mr. Balish's selection. If I chose to, I could grieve the decision. I spoke to Mr. Balish directly. He just told me that he had made the decision and that was that. I left. To grieve, or not to grieve, that was the question. I couldn't do that to Mr. Balish. So I put my pride aside and ended my quest to pursue a grievance against my principal. I knew Mr. Balish must have had his reasons for not selecting me. The school was still recovering from that devastating racial riot and Mr. Balish was probably trying to address some of the complaints from minority students, and their parents, who wanted to see more minorities in positions of authority. I felt I made the right decision because, as soon as there was another opening in the college office, Mr. Balish selected me.

However, I did receive a complaint about the new teacher from one of my female student aides which I reported to Mr. Balish. "Mrs. Farkouh, every time you go for lunch, the college advisor comes to your desk where I am doing my homework or doing some work for you, pulls down the window blinds next to your desk and proceeds to try to kiss me. If my Dad finds out, he will come to school and kill him!"

When I told Mr. Balish about the incident, he didn't say a word. However, the next day the window shades near my desk had been removed. I don't know if he spoke to the teacher but I do know that I had a happy camper working for me. Politics started to change in the late 1970s and that teacher would have been removed from the classroom immediately if the incident occurred in the 1980s. But when this incident occurred, it was too soon. In fact, if a female teacher (of course married) became pregnant, as soon as the principal found out, the next day she was dismissed. Not today. Politics, political climate, changes, changes, changes...

When the senior college advisor retired, Mr. Balish put me in charge of the college office. His previous appointee did not last too long. I never asked Mr. Balish about his discussion with the teacher or whatever happened concerning my student aide but, suffice to say, the teacher eventually left his position.

One day Mr. Balish came to my office and asked me what I needed. I asked for a full-time school secretary to help me with the clerical work. He appointed Marion Johnson for the college office. She was a talented school secretary with extraordinary skills. Like many school secretaries of her caliber, she had the qualities of an executive assistant. She helped with the typing of the student college applications, organized the office, and made it a pleasure for the college advisors, like myself, to work in small groups with all student grade levels. We advised ninth graders about perspective careers; continued to counsel tenth graders; prepared eleventh graders for investigating two and four-year colleges, as well as vocational careers; and helped twelfth graders with their final college and scholarship applications. Juniors and seniors, as well as their parents, were provided with information about the College Board as well as financial aid. I asked Mr. Balish if I could change the title of the office to College Career Office. What do you think his response was? You guessed it!

On another occasion, Mr. Balish dropped by the office and asked me if I wanted to get involved in an experimental program whereby five schools in the city would be involved with a search program that would help students not only make career choices, but help them search for two- and four-year colleges. I was very excited about Port Richmond High School being a pilot school. The other college advisor and I began to run financial aid and scholarship workshops in the evenings for students and parents. An endearing lady and best friend, Phyllis Simon, who was a new guidance counselor, helped me to run a freshmen career program. The students used the college and career search computer terminals and Phyllis would run small and individual guidance groups to follow-up with the career information that the students had retrieved. The College Advisors would discuss the students' lists of colleges with them and help them to make postsecondary decisions. That was the way it was. Mr. Balish, Phyllis, and I began an innovative program for high school students. Mr. Balish was able to get funds to support vocational and job programs so that those students interested in a vocational or work study program could use the resources in our office. An inspiring teacher by the name of Tony Brown was instrumental in the success of the program. Another key figure was Harvey Weber, dean of students. He worked closely with us to get the students who got into trouble to use our office for vocational and college information. Herbert Balish started to integrate program after program within the school. Port Richmond High School was making its mark in Staten Island. It had been one of the best high schools on the Island during the first five decades of its operation and now it was regaining that reputation, thanks to the efforts of outstanding educators like Herbert Balish.

During this period, our family had outgrown the small duplex on Jefferson Avenue. We started looking for a larger home and soon found a center-hall colonial house located in Sunset Hill on the North Shore of Staten Island. It had just been built and faced Silver Lake Golf Course. In fact, our house was right in front of the ninth hole in a lovely cul-de-sac. Charles and Stephen attended P.S. 45 and Cathy went to I.S. 61, as the boys did later. Cathy and Charles were sent to Susan Wagner High School because the Guidance Department at I.S. 61 did not send them to their feeder school, Curtis High School. All the kids on the block went to Susan Wagner High School until Curtis High School, their zoned school, realized that the I.S. 61 Guidance Department was not properly sending students to their zoned schools. Stephen and the rest of the students on Croton Avenue, as well as Herkimer Street, were then sent to Curtis High School. I believe the underlying reason for this error was definitely racial since Curtis High School was not the place to send white students! Well, it was the best thing to happen to Stephen. He received a wonderful education at Curtis High School and was able to grow up in a multi-racial school which truly reflected the real world. Stephen did exceptionally well and graduated third in his class from Curtis High School.

My educational experience continued as I worked at Port Richmond High School. I not only had a wonderful mentor as principal but, as I have mentioned, my mathematics chairman, Ike Feinberg, was my inspiration as well. He was most instrumental in developing my instructional skills. Ike was always there for me. Whenever I needed a motivation, I would go to him. He was disappointed when I became College Advisor because I had not confided in him about my desire to take a compensatory job. Nevertheless, I offered my expertise to help him with curriculum development and mentoring the younger, less experienced teachers. I had the utmost respect for his leadership and I was very fortunate to have him play a very important role in my career. I found myself often torn between helping in the Mathematics Department and developing special programs in the College Career Office. Mr. Balish and Ike were leaders in education far ahead of their generation. Ike gave me a solid foundation to build my educational career upon and Mr. Balish was the cement that held together my dream of aspiring to be an educational leader one day.

Mr. Balish taught me so much. Once, unannounced, he observed me in the classroom. At the end of the lesson, he came up to me as the students were leaving and said, "Alice, you have it. Now, flaunt it." Until today, almost forty years later, when I want to give a teacher or student encouragement, I retell the story about Mr. Balish's visit and what he said to me "You have it. Now flaunt it."

Yes, Mr. Balish began his mentoring of me in the 1970s but it didn't end. His influence in my educational career never ceased while he was alive and even after his untimely death . . . . Is this the end of the chapter of my life with Mr. Balish? Of course not! I am not finished with the story of this special colleague and friend. I will walk in his footsteps and in his shadow for the rest of my life and hope that I will pass the torch of leadership to those who follow me. My father once told me, "Alice, you can count your friends on one hand." At the time, I was very upset with this remark, and asked him, "What do you mean? I have only five friends." It took several years before I realized that my wise father knew I had more than five friends. True friends are rare. Herbert Balish was one of those friends which Dad told me I could count on one hand.

Chapter VII

My First Promotion

Life at Prospect Heights

On the summer of 1971, it was time to think about a second master's degree. The family was growing. Cathy was ten; Charles, eight; and Stephen, six. They were great children. Cathy loved her brothers and was "the big sister." Charles and Stephen respected her authority. If I got home late from a meeting, the supper table was set. I didn't have to tell them to start their homework. They knew their responsibilities. Each week, one of the children had a "kitchen responsibility." Their bedrooms were usually in order, with Cathy the neatest. My husband, Charlie, was very supportive of me as well. He helped me with the family and made life a little easier for a full-time working mom. So, now I was ready to go back to school but, of course, it would have to be in the evening and during the summer months. The New York City Board of Education required a raise in salary to be based on graduate study. I either had to earn 30 credits, pass the C2 Promotional Step, or earn another master's degree. Of course, it would be another master's degree. Should I pursue a degree in guidance, or in supervision and administration, or a third degree in mathematics? I loved all three areas but I decided to follow my role models, Ike and Mr. Balish, and learn how to help other teachers.

I started to pursue a Sixth Year Certification in Supervision and Administration at Richmond College (CUNY). After a short period of time, I earned the Certification in 1975 and was ready to apply for supervisory positions on the secondary level in New York City. At this point, there were no written examinations for the license. In the past, an assistant principal had to take a written examination in the discipline of supervision. A list of supervisors were ranked. The list was generated by rank so principals could pick their candidates from the list. As a result, I was in competition with a list of perspective supervisors who were on a "former examination" list. I was turned down on the first try for the position of Assistant Principal of Mathematics at Clara Barton High School in Prospect Heights, Brooklyn, because I wasn't on a "list." The school's principal had decided to select a male supervisor in mathematics who had to be on the supervisory list. He never said that, but I knew that was the reason. In addition, there were very few women aspiring to be supervisors of mathematics. After all, what did women know about mathematics?

On the second try, I applied to Prospect Heights High School located at 883 Clawson Avenue, which, ironically, was just across the street from Clara Barton High School. The original name for Prospect Heights was Girls' Commercial. It was the same school which my mother had attended as a freshman when it opened its doors in the late 1920's.

The principal of Prospect Heights was Robert Couche, a very bright and outspoken black educator. He was trying very hard to turn around a school that needed help desperately. I will never forget walking into his conference room for an interview. Seated at the desk were all female parents, Mr. Couche, and his able assistant. "Aha," I said to myself, "Maybe I have a chance." My colleagues at Port Richmond High School thought that I was crazy to apply to a troubled, all-black high school. I didn't want to tell them that my neighbors in my old neighborhood of Staten Island thought I was crazy to teach at a multiracial school like Port Richmond High School. Yet, I had had the greatest nine and a half

Robert Couche, principal of Prospect Heights High School, Brooklyn. I
remember him as a bright, outspoken, hard-working man who tried his
best to turn around a school that desperately needed help.
(Photo courtesy Prospect Heights High School Yearbook, Cardinal, 1976)

years of training as a teacher, and college and career advisor
while working there alongside my colleagues, especially Mr.
Balish, and Ike, not to mention other assistant principals like Walter, Beverly, Nick, John, Eileen, and Mike. I could go on and on
about my memorable experiences with students, parents, and
colleagues at Port Richmond High School, even though I know it
was difficult for a lot of people at the time to understand my love
for teaching minorities. I wanted to do something special for the
students of Prospect Heights High School. So, here I was at the
interview process. Was I nervous? You bet!

The parents, led by Mr. Couche, asked me pertinent questions
about curriculum, supervision, and teaching black youths. Then,
after the interview, Mr. Couche stood up and shook my hand. It
was not long before he called me up and congratulated me.
When I arrived the first day, Mr. Couche made a startling remark
to me. He said, "Alice, there is only one regret I have about hiring
you." "Well, what is that, Mr. Couche?" He quickly responded, "I

believe that you are overqualified to work here." In turn, I replied, "You will never be disappointed in hiring me. Your colleague across the street didn't accept me because I was not on a promotion list based on an earlier set of examinations. I couldn't take the examination because by the time I qualified for the test, it had been eliminated. You chose me for my ability and enthusiasm. I will make remarkable changes at Prospect Heights for you." He smiled at me, took my hand, and gently kissed it. I soon learned that Mr. Couche was not always gentle for he expected total respect from the students and staff and when either group stepped out of line, you heard about it. He wanted the best for his students and their parents. He wanted to turn the school around, and if you were not loyal to him, that was the end of his respect for you.

I was now the Assistant Principal of Mathematics at Prospect Heights High School. I couldn't wait to tell Mom about the school. After all, she attended the pristine school the day it opened its doors. I was surprised that Mom never wanted to come and visit the building. I didn't ask her why, but it was probably because the Depression Era took away her adolescent years and saddened her. I would tell her about the logistics of the building and she would listen intently with a tear or two in her eyes. She was proud of me and I wished that Dad was there, as well, to share my joy. Although I know that even if he wasn't there in body, he was there in spirit. He and Mom had both been anxious for me to become a teacher. Well, now I was a supervisor of mathematics. I had to teach three classes; supervise twenty-four teachers and three paraprofessionals; be a Mom for a fifteen, a thirteen and an eleven-year-old; be a wife, and take care of a three-bedroom home. I did it all with enthusiasm and love. Well, maybe not always with enthusiasm, for there were times after leaving at 6:45 a.m. and returning at 5:30 p.m. when I was weary. I put on twenty pounds and two dress sizes during my time at Prospect Heights.

From my first day at Prospect Heights High School, I so much wanted to be half as good as my mentor, Ike Feinberg, who had taught me how to be an effective teacher. Now, I was going to use all his leadership qualities to be an effective supervisor. I inherited a scholarly department. Most of the teachers in the mathematics department were excellent mathematicians and educators. The acting supervisor of the Mathematics Department had not been given the job because apparently Mr. Couche was not satisfied with his leadership. There may have been other reasons, but who was I to question Mr. Couche's decision as to why he had decided to replace this supervisor and appoint me on the first day of the spring term? When I finally met the previous supervisor, he mentioned to me that there had been a rumor that Mr. Couche gave me the job because I knew someone at the Board of Education. After a while though, I believe this man realized that I wasn't a "token female" but a qualified supervisor and educator who deserved the job.

One of the younger teachers under my supervision had just been assigned to the school. His name was Elliott Ringhel and he started the day after my arrival. Elliott was neatly dressed in a suit, white shirt and tie. He looked like a teenager and still does. I soon had him helping me clean up the mathematics office. What a mess! He reminded me almost thirty years later that I put him to work in the office on his first day. However, he will never forget that I sent him a thank you note the very next day. In fact he said, "You did that all the time. You always appreciated us." Well, of course, that was how we were brought up as children. We were told to respect others and remember to work as hard as you would expect others to work for you. Otherwise, don't ask others to do a job that you wouldn't do yourself.

My first year at Prospect Heights was spent getting to learn the strengths and weaknesses of the mathematics teachers, as well as other key members of the school; placing the students properly as they entered the school from the Caribbean Islands and feeder schools; redesigning the curriculum so that more

challenging courses could be offered to the student body; training teachers to redesign the curriculum guides and courses of
study; getting a tutorial center set up during the lunch periods;
and learning to gain the respect of a divided group of mathematics teachers, as well as a divided faculty in general. I started a
Mathematics Club at the school, too. The easiest part of my job
was being with the students. Most of them were kind and warm.
They yearned to learn and better themselves. My biggest challenge was convincing school personnel that the educational
background of our students from the Caribbean Islands was not
as bad as Americans thought it was. It was so sad to see so many
bright students placed in classes that they were overqualified for.
They knew their arithmetic skills well and performed
higher-level skills. They accepted academic challenges, and were
able to synthesize and analyze complex problems. What was very
interesting is that they loved to show me or their teachers how
they were taught mathematics in their countries. Almost all the
students in the school came from disadvantaged homes. As a result, they were mandated to be Title I students and given
remediation classes in mathematics and English. This was in spite
of the fact that they were tested and many scored a twelfth-grade
level in both reading and mathematics. Mr. Couche gave me his
approval to make changes in the placement of students.

I noticed that the majority of students wore their coats all day
in the fall and winter because they were afraid of them being stolen. Fear of poverty was so noticeable at the school. But it meant
that I had to add hygiene to the mathematics curriculum in my
geometry class. Those woolen coats had to come off during the
winter months! They complied with my request, removed their
coats and hung them up in class. Physical education teachers del-
icately handled the issue of personal hygiene. However, we did
not know how they lived when they returned to their homes after the school day. Did they have the money to purchase ade-
quate hygienic items? We weren't in control after the school day
ended. However, we were with them during the day to be their

teachers, mentors, and most of all, their friends. Do we really know what awaits a disadvantaged student when they spend a day in a warm, nourishing climate at school and then go home to poverty and the cold?

I will never forget what happened one day when I had visitors from various careers speak to the students in my Mathematics Club after the school day. I had received a beautiful attaché suitcase as a farewell gift from the Mathematics Department at Port Richmond High School. My initials, ABF, were engraved on the handle plate. I had placed my lesson plan books and papers that I needed to take home in the case and locked the office door. When I returned to my office after the career meeting at the Mathematics Club, I found my office broken into and my attaché case stolen. I cried all the way home. I reconvened the Mathematics Club the following afternoon. I informed them that I always go the extra mile and think about them. I informed them that during the meeting the day before, my office had been broken into and my attaché case stolen. I didn't want the papers returned, but I did want the case back. Spread the word and tell your friends that no questions will be asked. Just tell whoever was involved to place the case outside my office. The following day, about 3:30 p.m., the case was sitting outside my office. All the contents were there. I was so proud of the Club members, as well as the thief. Well, a little bit proud of the thief. It just shows that there is good even in a thief. Students knew right from wrong and they respected and cared about people who cared about them.

The next few years were spent on being the best supervisor I could be.

Mr. Couche would critique my observation reports with a fine-tooth comb. He was a very bright and capable principal. His eloquent speeches, coupled with the respect he had at the principal meetings throughout the Board of Education, were just a few positive attributes he possessed. However, he still continued to fight the bureaucracy at the Board. He wanted urinals for the boys' bathrooms since the school was originally only to have girls. When the name was changed and the school was opened to boys, there were no plans to have urinals for the young men. That was not acceptable to Mr. Couche.

The School Safety Division was created around this time and its officers were required to wear uniforms. This move to up-grade the dignity of the position was initiated by a former physical education teacher, and friend and colleague of mine, Angelo Aponte. He had worked as a substitute teacher and basketball coach at Port Richmond High School many years ago. He was one of the "shining stars" in the Board of Education. Angelo thought "outside of the box" during the late 1970s when very few did. He was creative, innovative, and one of those rare individuals who was really improving our education system. He continued to put the School Safety Division on the map and even earned a Juris Doctorate Degree along the way.

We were aware that criminal activity was going on within the Prospect Heights' school gates. Despite the security guards, drug dealers were still making it through the school's side exits, and selling drugs to our students. So, Mr. Couche took care of the door problem. He chained all doors except for the main entrance so thieves and drug dealers could not enter. He was fined so many times by the Fire Department that there came a point when he realized that the Board was not addressing his needs as a strict disciplinarian and caring principal. I am sure he had other issues with the teachers union, as well as school personnel, which weighed on his mind but he chose not to discuss these matters with us at the senior staff meetings. I guess he felt it was his war. He once told the cabinet that, "Prospect Heights was like a woman. Once she earned a bad name, she would always keep it. The only way to change was to change the name." The name didn't change and, no matter how hard he tried, Prospect Heights was not considered a school that students would want to come to for a good education.

Prospect Heights continued to be known as one of the most undesirable high schools in the city. It was completely segregated. There were only black students throughout the school. I once witnessed a guidance counselor discouraging white students from attending the school. Was a segregated school, with separate but equal education, considered constitutional? I thought that was taken care of by the U.S. Supreme Court's landmark decision in 1954 with *Brown v. the Board of Education of Topeka.* I understood that, "Separate but Equal" was unconstitutional. Then why was Prospect Heights allowed to exist under "separate but equal" status if the top court of our country constitutionally overruled it? Show me any high school in the system, from the 1970s up to the present, that is segregated and I'll prove to you that it is not an effective school or a school which many parents desire for their children. Many of the schools in the NYC Board of Education which remained segregated, like Prospect Heights High School, ultimately closed down to be reconfigured into "small magnet or specialized schools." This is what happened to Prospect Heights in 2006.

To our surprise, Robert Couche gave up "his battle" and decided to retire in June 1979. That was very sad for me. Although it was not easy working with a strong disciplinarian, I highly respected and loved the man and knew when he left we were going to be in big trouble. We sure were!

An acting principal ran the school until Miss Wilhelmina A. Young, a former Assistant Principal of Physical and Health Education, was appointed to replace Mr. Couche. She appeared capable and was extremely friendly towards me. She asked me to be her Mistress of Ceremonies at her installation. I accepted. I continued to work hard. I even started the first Advanced Placement Calculus course at Prospect Heights. Arthur Green, the Coordinator of Student Affairs (COSA) at Prospect Heights, was a dear friend. He helped me to assimilate into the culture of the school. I will never forget his advice, wisdom, and support. I remember on one particular occasion he spoke to me after he had seen me in

In this picture, I am in my classroom reviewing the mathematics honor roll list with Arthur Green, the Coordinator of Student Affairs at Prospect Heights High School. Arthur became a dear friend and helped me assimilate into the culture of the school when I was Assistant Principal of Mathematics from 1977-81.

the cafeteria at lunch disciplining some students who were misbehaving, "Do you know who you were reprimanding in the cafeteria last period?" In my opinion, it didn't matter who I was talking to, if the student did not act properly, I would speak to him or her about the issue. I replied, "No." Arthur informed me that the student was a known member of a street gang and probably would not think twice about slashing my throat. Well, I continued to be myself since I couldn't change my beliefs, only my place of employment.

I also ran into problems with the school's Assistant Principal of Administration when I requested a room adjacent to the cafeteria so I could run a Tutorial Center for students who needed math help. He would not give permission for the use of the classroom and when I asked him for a reason he told me, "Alice, do you want the other assistant principals to be jealous of you because we gave you a special room?" I replied that I didn't think that would happen since no other department planned to tutor students during the lunch period. His unprofessional manner in dealing with my request meant that my students in the Mathematics Department continued to be tutored in the cafeteria while mashed potatoes and corn and peas were thrown at them, on a daily basis, during their tutoring sessions. This same administrator even went so far as to limit all Assistant Principals of Supervision to a fixed number of copies that could be run off on the copier machine in his office, and all of us had to use the obsolete rexo-machines. Supervision, in his opinion, was secondary to administration. He had a bright wife who became the assistant principal of another discipline. Unfortunately, a husband and wife could not be in the same school when both were supervisors. So who left? The competent and highly respected wife left.

The Mathematics Department continued to work hard. I was able to get the teachers to work together as a team. The Title I students were those who were poor or who lived in a low-income area. We were mandated by the city, state, and federal governments to give them remediation courses. After carefully testing them, I got Miss Young's permission to take many of them out of remediation and placed them in higher level courses such as tenth, eleventh, and twelfth year mathematics, as well as Advanced Placement Calculus. What were students with 12.0 reading and mathematics grade levels doing in Fundamental Mathematics and Math Lab classes? This was a degrading way to treat bright young men and women! It was a struggle, but we removed them from remediation classes. One student in my geometry class earned a 100 on the Geometry Regents. I approached another young student, who excelled in my class, about her career choices. When I asked her what she was interested in doing, she responded that she wanted to be a nurse. I asked her, "Why not a doctor?" She stared at me and replied, "You are the first person to tell me that." I don't know what she ended up doing, but I would bet my last dollar that she took my advice. Many of

To Mrs FARKOUH
A beautiful lady full of
Courage and determination.
One of the sweetest teachers
any student could ask for.
You are truly a Great teacher
not only in your methods but
due to the facts that you care
greatly about the wellfare of your students.
Beleive me, 99% of your students love and
respect you.
I love and respect you too
Granville.

'80

I treasured this note from Granville, a graduating
senior at Prospect Heights in 1980, because I always
wanted my students to know that I was their
champion, and I encouraged all of them to reach for
their dreams, and aspire to whatever occupation
they desired.

Prospect Heights High School former students became successful
chemical and civil engineers and CEOs of successful
organizations.

Once a year, I had the Advanced Placement Calculus class
visit my home. I invited them over the day after Christmas and
they always had a great time. They brought their ethnic Black
Cake, which was a delicious Caribbean rum fruit cake. I baked
them apple pie, brownies, homemade ziti, garlic bread, and other
goodies. Most of them had never seen or eaten Italian food. They
dressed up in suits and ties, party dresses and high heels. They
spent the entire day with me and didn't want to leave. We would
work awhile on the new Mathematics Department magazine,
Prospect Pyramid, which, during my time at the school, won
awards twice in the Columbia Scholastic Press competition. Not
the medalist award, but second place. Still, it was a beginning. I
remember one of the young people who came to my home

during Christmas later called me to say he was forever grateful to me for opening up my home to the class, being their champions, and encouraging them to aspire to whatever occupation they desired.

I will never forget the time when the Mathematics Club took a trip to Great Adventure, an amusement park in New Jersey. The Assistant Principal of Physical Education and I were in charge of a bus load of young people who had never been to an amusement park. When we got to Great Adventure, we instructed the students to stay in groups of five or six and not to stray outside of the park. In addition, we reminded the class that they were to report back to the bus no later than 5:30 p.m. Well, it was 6:00 p.m. and one student was missing. After waiting for half an hour, I decided to go to the security station and report the missing student. When I arrived at the security station, they informed me that it was the park's policy not to make any announcements over the loudspeaker about a lost child. After my "usual persuasion," I got them to make my announcement. I was happy, but a little embarrassed as the announcement was made, "Will Kirk Douglas please report to the school bus. Your teachers are waiting for you." Yes, that was his real name—Kirk Douglas, just like the Hollywood movie star! Kirk quietly shuffled onto the bus as I followed him. He told me that he was having so much fun and didn't realize that the time had passed so quickly. Well, guess who sat next to him all the way home and gave him a long lecture?

We had social times and we had "getting down to the essentials times." I got parents to come to the P.A. meetings in the evening by inviting them to see their children honored when they were enrolled in the Mathematics Department Honor and Merit Rolls. I had a very capable Title I Coordinator, Alice White, and Title I Supervisor, Irene Gross. Alice was my right arm, helping to make sure that Title I guidelines were followed and students were placed properly. Irene was instrumental in helping us to improve the student scores on the city examinations. The Preliminary Competency Examination (PCT) was established in the late

1970s, and we were in the forefront working on curriculum, placement, and raising achievement levels.

In spite of improving the Mathematics Department, it was not enough. Many parents were still not coming to P.A. meetings at night, fights continued to break out among the students, and faculty and student morale continued to decline. Prospect Heights had very few extracurricular activities for its students. Where were the steel bands, academic classes, and sports teams? Where were activities for students to excel in and raise school spirit? We were very lucky to have a talented and bright Assistant Principal of Social Studies, Dr. Marvin Barksdale, who was well-loved by the students; and a great Coordinator of Student Affairs, Arthur Green; and a gifted and bright Assistant Principal of Art, Elliott Thorne. Unfortunately, this was not enough. The school still did not move up in its academic standings. My good friend, Saul Lander, the Science Assistant Principal, decided to leave. Two Assistant Principals of Guidance came and went, and the Assistant Principal of Physical Education retired. Our male students never got their urinals, there wasn't a viable music program, and new computers came in the delivery entrance and went out the "back door." Things didn't get better. School spirit was low in spite of the many dedicated teachers who tried.

Graffiti soon became the thing to do. It got so bad to the point where the principal gave me a spray can of graffiti cleaner and asked that the students clean up the graffiti from their desks. I wouldn't let my students do this because the spray was very toxic. I went and spoke to the principal about my concerns. Her reply stunned me. "Then, Farkouh, you clean the desks off." When I told her I wouldn't, she grabbed the can from my hands, opened a file drawer and threw it inside. That was the moment when I made the decision to leave Prospect Heights after over four years of devoted service.

I decided to apply to Curtis High School back in Staten Island when there was a position open. It was only ten minutes away from my home and my younger son, Stephen, was just completing his sophomore year at the high school. I spoke to the principal of Prospect Heights, and she assured me that she would "not get in my way" for the lateral move. I applied like every other candidate and went through Level I, Level II, and a classroom observation at Curtis High School. There were about 20 other candidates in the classroom when we observed a lesson. Since I was the only one there who had four and a half years experience as an appointed Assistant Principal of Supervision, I blew the other candidates away. By the time the lesson ended, I had a written observation in hand. One of the candidates was David Whitebook. He was the COSA and mathematics teacher at Fort Hamilton High School. He had been sitting next to me and later told me that when he looked over at me at the end of the observation he couldn't believe that I had not only taken notes but had finished a rough draft of an observation for the entire lesson! That came from four and a half years experience of observing teachers at Prospect Heights.

It was time for Level III of the interview. Then, I got a call from the Superintendent of BASIS (Brooklyn and Staten Island Schools) informing me that I was not eligible to apply since I needed a half-year more for an administrative transfer. "Transfer, what transfer?" I couldn't believe that he would let me go through two levels of interviews and a classroom observation and afterwards tell me that I was ineligible to apply. "Never say can't . . . . never say can't . . . ." He was truly mistaken. I informed him that I had not filed for a transfer. I followed the same process as the other candidates. His decision was probably based on another reason. After hanging up, it came to me that probably my principal was waiting to see how I progressed before she stopped the process. Little did she realize that I made it straight to the top. I got help from Lester Golden, the President of the Association of Assistant Principals of Supervision, as well as someone from the Chancellor's Office. End result, I was assigned to Curtis High School as of September, 1981 as the newly appointed Assistant Principal of Mathematics. The Superintendent of BASIS was not a happy camper. In fact, this was an understatement! He remarked to my good friend, Phyllis Simon, as I found out many years later, that "Alice was crazy to do what she did, but she is probably the best Assistant Principal of Mathematics in the City of New York." I don't know if I would go as far as that because the Mathematics Chairmen Association (MCA), later on to be known as the Association of Mathematics Assistant Principals Supervision (AMAPS), had many outstanding supervisors. That's why Ike was my model! He and many other supervisors in the organization exemplified the fine qualities that I modeled myself upon during my career as a mathematics teacher and supervisor. Until today, AMAPS is considered a prestigious organization in the NYC Department of Education dedicated to excellence in mathematics for all students.

Well, I was on my way to Curtis High School. It was sad that I couldn't say good-bye to my students at Prospect Heights High School, but I left a part of my heart at that school. I had trained Elliott Ringhel as my replacement. He is no longer at the school but transferred to another high school. The bad news for Prospect Heights was that, as of June 2006, its doors closed forever. However, I know that its history, dating back to the 1920s, will never be forgotten.

I didn't formally say good-bye to my department at Prospect Heights. So, during the fall of 1981, I arranged to have everyone over to my home for supper. I made sure that the teachers who were Orthodox Jews, and comprised about 50 percent of the department, would be served kosher food in a separate area of the house. I also invited close colleagues from other departments at Prospect Heights as well. We had a wonderful time. My heritage has taught me to be a brother and sister to all around me. It is unfortunate that my Lebanese-Syrian upbringing was not a way of life for us all in today's climate, especially in the Middle East where tension still prevails. Perhaps the spirit of the Mathematics Department at Prospect Heights High School is a fine example of how people could co-exist in the world today. I humbly thank my family for bringing us up in a manner that has influenced our lives and we hope will continue for generations to come.

I will never forget my endearing friends at Prospect Heights. Principal Robert Couche gave me the opportunity to enter the "male-dominated" world of administrators. Educators such as Mr. Couche, Dr. Marvin Barksdale, Elliott Thorne, Saul Lander, Ann Sorrensen, Arthur Green, Marty Klein, Dorel Salner, Elliott Ringhel, Sylvia Beekman, Ruth Trencher, Irene Gross, Laverne North, Alice White, Anna Crichlow, Abe Bernstein, and John Economos will always have a special place in my heart. But it was time to move on to a new chapter in my life. On September 1, 1981, I began my new job as the Assistant Principal of Mathematics at Curtis High School in Staten Island.

Chapter VIII

Back to Staten Island

Curtis High School

Curtis High School stood like a queen on an elevated site that commanded a panoramic view of Upper New York Bay. It was Staten Island's first public secondary school and remained the only high school from 1904 until 1930. Located at 105 Hamilton Avenue in St. George, this regal and majestic building is one of the cherished landmarks of the borough of Staten Island. Upon my arrival in late June 1981, Principal Mitchell Schulich greeted me with enthusiasm. Apparently, he was not too happy with the former mathematics supervisor and knew that I would bring my expertise and experience to his school. Angelo, my dear friend from Port Richmond High School and Prospect Heights High School, had recommended me to Mr. Schulich.

So here I was. A little frazzled from the experience I had with the BASIS superintendent which left me with the feeling that I'd better "prove myself" at Curtis. As a Curtis High School parent, I had a wonderful experience with the teachers and the instructional programs of the school. My son, Stephen, had just completed his first year at the school and was a student in the Honors Academy. I had asked Stephen if he would feel uncomfortable about my applying to Curtis High School. On the contrary, he was overjoyed! Stephen ranked in the top 1% of the freshmen

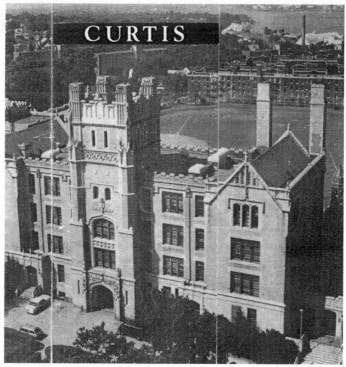

This is one of my favorite pictures of Curtis High School because it shows the full majesty of the school's architecture. I used this photo for a school pamphlet I designed in 1985.

class, so I guess that was one of the main reasons for my easy transition from parent to supervisor at the school.

During the summer of 1981, I worked closely with two experienced and dedicated mathematics teachers, Laney and Millie. They, too, were true friends. The kind that I could count on one hand, as my father had told me. Laney spent almost her entire summer vacation helping me to literally clean up the mathematics office. I entered the mathematics office to find a deluge of dirt, smelly opened tuna fish cans, tobacco, and whatever. The secured closet had papers and records dating back to the dark ages. The departmental files, including unofficial and confidential documents, were accessible to anyone who had a key to the office. The book room was a total mess. It was full of obsolete textbooks. Laney suggested that we use capable honor students to organize the bookshelves and take an inventory. To my dismay, current textbooks were not in supply for the opening of school in the fall.

As we cleaned up and organized the office, Laney proudly showed me around the computer room. She was ahead of her time. She started a computer program at the school when very few schools in the city had even thought about it. The room reflected Laney's organizational skills and interest in mathematics and computer science. Computers were neatly set up in an organized manner throughout the room. Charts of students' accomplishments and colorful computer-designed signs decorated the bulletin boards. Computer data files and textbooks were secured for the summer in a few student lockers. This was 1981. Very few schools had a workable computer classroom, let alone a teacher who was skilled in the BASIC computer language. There was no such title as a teacher licensed in computer science—Laney was unique.

Computer science was on the verge of being recognized as a new entity in high school education. Stephen was under Laney's tutelage and he was one of many students who helped her with the computer room during their lunch period. She had old TRS and Commodore computers. It didn't take long for Laney to make me realize that the school needed to purchase more state-of-the-art computers. Of course, the Board of Education didn't allot funds for computer education. In spite of this, Mr. Schulich did provide allowances to have computer classes and textbooks. However, the computers were becoming outdated very quickly. The students did an excellent job in programming and learning the BASIC computer language and graphics on the computers that were available.

As the years unfolded, we were able to buy new Apple IIe and AppleIIC computerpage. Students learned BASIC, ASCII, FORTRAN, and Advanced Placement Pascal thanks to the efforts of talented and scholarly teachers like Aurelia Curtis, who was hired by me in 1984. Aurelia came from Liberia and was the valedictorian of her high school. She designed and wrote the higher-level computer curriculums. When I eventually left in 1989, she kept up with computer languages and went on to teach C++, the language which eventually replaced Pascal. Because of Laney, students learned how to write original programs in the BASIC language, create and sort programs for businesses, and write graphic design computer programs.

During her lunch period, you would often find Laney in her computer room with ten or more students working at their computers, getting tutored by Laney, or just hanging around their favorite computer teacher. It just seemed like yesterday when the mathematics departments sold candles, Tupperware, pot holders, candy, candy, and candy. Why? They needed updated computers to keep up with the pace of advances in this newly emerging technology. I still remember Stephen selling carton after carton of M&M's candy to help purchase new computer equipment. That is, I thought he was selling the candy, until one day and many cartons later, I noticed the empty cartons and candy boxes stored under his bed and in his closet. He would eat the candy and have his father write out checks for the purchases. It was amazing that he didn't have a single cavity!

Mr. Schulich never questioned me when I needed something. He knew I worked above and beyond the school day, and was striving to improve student achievement scores on the New York State academic competency tests, Regents and RCTs (Regents Competency Tests, formerly known as BCTs). The other Assistant Principals at Curtis were extremely supportive of me. To help me out the first semester at Curtis High School, Fred and Pat (supervisors of the Science and English Departments) shared their textbook funds so I could order more up-to-date textbooks. I was also able to borrow books from my colleagues at Port Richmond High School. Within a few years, the Regents scores increased considerably; the new Mathematics magazine, *Curtis Cubic*, won Medalists Awards in the Columbia Scholastic Press Association competition. The Mathematics Department was now recognized for its excellence while the computer program,

| Aurelia Curtis—appointed principal of Curtis High School in 2003. | Tim (Timothy M.) Gannon —appointed principal of Port Richmond High School in 2005. |

My colleagues at Curtis High School, Aurelia Curtis and Tim Gannon, helped contribute to many of the fond memories I still have of my time there as a teacher and assistant principal from1981-89. These two dedicated teachers now enjoy successful careers of their own as high school principals. Congratulations!
(Photos courtesy Curtis High School and Port Richmond High School 2009)

headed by Laney, also excelled. Feeder schools worked with us in properly placing our students as they entered Curtis. The Mathematics Department grew from fewer than six teachers to almost twenty. Mr. Schulich gave us two paraprofessionals to help administer the Pupils with Compensatory Educational Needs (PCEN) classes and the Computer Program. Laney and I began to train Valerie, our first paraprofessional. As the years passed, Valerie became one of my best friends—you know, one of those few friends you can count on one hand. The Mathematics Department had talented teachers.

Teachers such as Laney, Millie, Frank, Sid, Aurelia, Tim, Richie, Al, Jim, and Art were examples of outstanding mathematics educators who truly cared about their job. Frank and Sid went on to become Assistant Principals after I left Curtis High School. Aurelia, bright, energetic and caring, began her career as a teacher and returned many years later as the principal of Curtis

High School. Her students, parents, faculty, and staff recognized her fine attributes and know that they are in excellent hands. Tim Gannon is also doing an excellent job as principal of Port Richmond High School. He leads with a strong and caring hand. This wonderful group of teachers and administrators will always have a special place in my heart.

Around 1985, I began to think about personal advancement. I took the NYC Principal's Examination and passed it on the first try. In those days, the Board of Education returned to the use of a written and oral examination for licensing assistant principals and principals. Now I was a licensed secondary principal on a list of candidates for promotion. What was the next step? The Board of Education decided to include me in a mentoring program in 1985—1986. In the fall of 1985, I participated once a week in a special program where sixteen assistant principals and central supervisors were mentored by experienced administrators from the Central Board of Education. In the spring of 1986, I was selected to work with a highly respected and talented school supervisor, Milton Mellor, who was principal of Canarsie High School in Brooklyn. Mr. Schulich agreed with my recommendation to place Frank Meringolo in my position while I stayed at Canarsie High School as Milton Mellor's "shadow."

Milton and his Assistant Principals of Guidance and Administration helped me. I followed Milton everywhere (except to the bathroom) and learned from him. One day, he asked me to do him a favor. It seemed that the deli across the street had a sign posted outside advertising, "Last stop for beer." Milton went on to say, "See if you can get them to remove it." "Okay." I put my coat on and went across the street to "chew the fat" with the owner. After a while, I returned. As I crossed the street, I couldn't help but look back. The owner was removing the sign. Milton was shocked. "What did you say to him?" I calmly told him, "Oh, that my daughter was marrying an Italian in August. I also casually mentioned how concerned we were to see a sign encouraging beer drinking across from a high school. Milton, he apologized to me and that was it." Milton thanked me and walked away. As my mentoring principal, he showed me how to observe music, shop, academic classes, and physical/health education classes. He also made me realize that a principal worked from early in the morning to late in the evening. There was a very different code of ethics for an effective principal and I was going to learn that from Milton. His work ethos soon became mine. That was what had to happen if I wanted to be principal. When I completed my five-month mentorship with Milton, staff members gave me a crystal owl and told me that it reminded them of me—"Wise as an owl." I will always cherish the memories of the five months with them and the invaluable mentoring given to me by Milton and his two assistant principals.

A few months later, I applied for principalship at Fort Hamilton High School—the school that I graduated from in 1957. I did not get the position. There were two endearing friends who helped me move on from this big disappointment. The first one was Milton who called me up when he heard how hard I was taking it. I will never forget the advice he gave me. "Alice, I know you are disappointed in not getting the principalship for Fort Hamilton. However, don't be hasty and accept any school job as principal. You may be given different offers or encouraged to apply to a school that is not the best for you. If you don't want to go there, don't apply for the school in the first place. Think of the *quality of your life*. That is more important than anything. You'll be principal one day, but just don't apply to any school."

When soon afterwards I was offered the position of principal at a high school in the Bronx—so far away from Staten Island, so far away from my family. I took Milton's advice: I declined the position. The Brooklyn Superintendent asked me to come to Prospect Heights as acting principal. I told her that they needed a black principal, not me. She responded with the words, "No, Farkouh, they don't need a black principal, they need someone like you." I was honored that she told me that because she herself was a dedicated black educator. I will forever be grateful to her for boosting my confidence, but I disagreed with her, for I thought that the best leader for Prospect Heights needed to be black. Maybe I was wrong. I will never know. However, one thing I will remember her for is that she respected me for what I was, helped me throughout my career when I needed support, and was always in the shadows ready to help me when I needed her. Her name was Joyce Coppin. Thank you, Joyce Coppin. You gave me hope and inspiration. Perhaps, if Mr. Couche was alive, maybe I would have returned to Prospect Heights High School.

The other friend was Valerie. She sent me a bouquet of flowers after she knew that I hadn't gotten the job at Fort Hamilton. On the card she wrote, "God loves you." That made me feel so good about remaining at Curtis. I told Mr. Schulich that I wouldn't leave him just to become a principal anywhere. I would stay at Curtis and continue to help the school out. He smiled and said, "Alice, thank you." I will never forget his humble thank you. He taught me humility and the steadfastness one needs when things don't go the way you want them to go. One other occasion that exemplifies his care for those around him is the time I had a medical emergency. I had a serious problem on a Friday afternoon, headed home, packed a suitcase, and drove immediately to the emergency room of St. Vincent's Hospital on Castleton and Bard Avenue in Staten Island. I was operated on Saturday. On Sunday, who walks into my room but Mr. Schulich with an African violet plant. He came to visit me! What an honor! By the way, the emergency was taken care of and the doctor said I could return to work. To my husband's dismay, I returned the following Monday. My husband said, "I knew you would pick a weekend to get sick."

I continued at Curtis for three more years. In 1987, Mr. Schulich had to take a few months off for health reasons. He selected me to be the acting principal until his return. I was absolutely thrilled. For the next two months, I was the acting principal. I wanted Mr. Schulich to be proud of me. Frank took my place once again and supervised the Mathematics

Department. I started observing teachers, meeting with parents, attending basketball games, and dealing with the politicians and other community leaders. I really got my feet wet. Then my bubble broke. Mr. Schulich gave me three days' notice that he was returning. I was shocked that he recuperated so fast. But, it was indeed his school. The entire faculty held a party for me the next day. They played "Camelot" and lined up one by one to tell me what a great principal I was. This was the best training I could have received. It was Mr. Schulich who gave me the opportunity to prove to my superiors that I was capable of being an effective leader of a high school. Thank you, Mr. Schulich, for the opportunity to show what kind of job I could do as a principal. I was blessed. Nevertheless, I still remained at Curtis.

My professional life didn't advance without Mr. Balish coming in and out of my daily life at school. At this point, Mr. Balish had the title of Deputy Superintendent while he was principal of Tottenville High School, on Staten Island's south shore. He planned effective and useful principal and administrative workshops at High School Division. It was at one workshop held at Teachers College, that I met an educator who would have a profound influence on me for the rest of my life. It was Dr. Frank Smith, Jr., creator and coordinator of the Inquiry Program at Columbia University. With a little push from Mr. Balish, I decided to go for a doctorate in Educational Administration at Teachers College. I was going to get my doctorate and apply for principal positions outside of New York City. I was accepted and started my course work while at Curtis High School.

The Inquiry Program was a special program that attracted educators from all over the United States. Classes were held on weekends during the school year and over two summers. While still at Curtis High School, I started the first year of study. I loved it, but I did not know that the start of the Inquiry Program would connect me with the great educators who worked at Teachers College, Columbia University, and offer me the opportunity to learn about different educators, school systems, and school programs throughout the United States. What a wonderful experience. I will forever be grateful to Mr. Balish and Dr. Frank Smith, Jr. for their support and encouragement to go for the gold ring. I was going to be a principal one day and not principal of "just any school." At the time, one of my colleagues told me that "I was too old to be a principal" for after all, I was in my late 40s. Too old, she's got to be kidding . . . . never say can't . . . . never say can't.

Then one afternoon on my way home from the summer program at Teachers College, Charlie picked me up at the St. George's Ferry, in Staten Island. He started laughing and said, "Guess what?" I laughed and responded, "Chancellor Green has called me up and offered me a principalship somewhere." Charlie chuckled and said, "No, this is better news. The principal at Fort Hamilton High School has resigned and the school needs a new principal." I couldn't believe it. I always wanted to return to Fort Hamilton, my alma mater, as a mathematics teacher. I never dreamt that I now had a second chance to return as the principal.

The BASIS Superintendent selected Nick Coletto to be the Interim Principal. Nick would hold this position for only one year and would not be allowed to apply for the permanent position. This ruling had been instituted by Chancellor Richard Green since so many interim positions had been reversed to permanent positions, giving the acting principal the inside track. I called Herbert Balish and asked him if I should apply for Fort Hamilton High School once again. I will always remember his words, "Alice, strike the anvil while the iron is hot. It is your school." I couldn't wait to update my application and submit it to High School Division. I knew I would be among many qualified candidates competing for the principalship; however, I was not going to give up. Don't tell me I can't do something when I am determined. I grew up in Bay Ridge, the area where the school was located. I was an American of Lebanese, Syrian and Greek heritage. The area of Bay Ridge had always been my home. In spite of the fact that we moved to Staten Island in 1963, Charlie and I had traveled to church every Sunday in Bay Ridge via the 69th Street Ferry until 1964 when the Verrazano-Narrows Bridge opened. We were married in St. Mary's Church, just a few blocks away from Fort Hamilton High School, and our three children were baptized at St. Mary's. I was going to have the opportunity to link my two communities of Bay Ridge and Staten Island. Fort Hamilton High School was going to be "my school one day." I could feel it in my bones.

I attended PTA meetings at Fort Hamilton High School, read the school profile, visited the school and spoke to assistant principals, as well as Nick Colleto. I talked to parents in and outside of the school whose children either graduated from the school or currently attended the school. Since my church was just two blocks away from Fort Hamilton High School, I was able to get firsthand information about what the community thought about the school. My husband and I were alumni of the school, but I was not actively involved. Charlie was on the Executive Board of the Fort Hamilton High School Alumni Association, but he felt that he could not be involved in any meetings or decisions to recommend me since that was a conflict of interest on his part. That was Charlie, fair and just. It is qualities like these which I have always admired in him. He has not only been a special husband, but my confidant when I needed an honest opinion, even if I didn't agree with him.

I had been given a plaque by the Fort Hamilton High School Alumni Association in 1986 in recognition of my contributions in Education and the Community Life of Bay Ridge. I was active in the Board of Trustees at St. Mary's Church, and the Superintendent of its Church School, as well as the Assistant Principal of Prospect Heights. Other than that, I stood on my own attributes.

On the day I was interviewed by a committee of parents and members of the Superintendent's Office, as well as Dr. Kriftcher, the superintendent, I decided to wear my FHHS school ring. There had been a snow storm the previous day and I needed to drive up three treacherous hills and down one winding hill to get

My appointment as principal of Fort Hamilton High School became
effective on May 1, 1989. I was returning to my alma mater as the first
woman in its history to head the school. In this photo, I am standing at
the school's front entrance shortly after I officially began as principal.
(Photo courtesy Steve Zaffarano, Staten Island Advance 1989)

to Clove Road so that I could get onto the expressway and over
the Verrazano-Narrows Bridge into Bay Ridge. My car slid and
skidded all over the place. I couldn't get off the block. My housekeeper and good friend, Anne, pulled out her car keys and told
me to use her car. It would give me good luck. I swung her car
into gear and off I went, ring and all. I made it to the interview on
time. Anne has always been and will always be a wonderful
friend to me. My Scottish and loving friend to our family was
"our Annie."

My school ring reminded me of Fort Hamilton's school spirit
back in the late 1950s. I was being interviewed for a different Fort
Hamilton High School. It was a school with almost no school
spirit. Fort Hamilton's status in the community was dwindling. It
had been placed on the SUR (School Under Review) list by the
New York State Education Department for the last few years because of dwindling attendance and poor reading and

mathematics scores. The interim principal, as well as the former principal, had worked hard in trying to upgrade programs, student achievement, and student attendance. They were making some headway, but not enough. The school was removed from the SUR list in 1987 but there were still serious concerns at the school. It was also scheduled to be renovated and a state-of-the-art natatorium (indoor pool complex) was to be built. I still wanted to be principal. After three levels of interviews, I was called by Dr. Kriftcher and informed that as of May 1, I would be assigned as the newly appointed principal of Fort Hamilton High School. I was once again on the move. Nine and a half years at Port Richmond High School, four and a half years at Prospect Heights High School, eight years at Curtis High School and now, finally, on May 1, 1989, I would become the newly appointed principal of my alma mater.

Curtis High School had a farewell party for me in the elegant library. The faculty gave me a beautiful Waterford clock and the Mathematics Department gave me an exquisite piece of Spanish porcelain from the Lladró collection. One of my mathematics teachers, Millie Rogan, had been responsible for selecting it. She told me that the figurine they chose reminded her of "the lady with a vision." I placed it in our family room and have never moved it since. I am reminded every day of my wonderful friendships and relationships with students, parents, and faculty at Curtis High School. That is what education and teaching are all about. On my last day at Curtis, I was attempting to leave quietly from the side exit, when I heard a voice in the background. It was one of my teachers, Tim Gannon. He ran up to me and gave me a good-bye kiss. At this point, tears of sadness ran down my cheeks. "Tim," I remember saying, "You did it, Tim. I was sure I could make it out of this building without a tear, but now you did it." I would miss them all: Laney, Millie, Valerie, Aurelia, Tim, Art, Richie, Frank, Al, Jim, Sid, and Lynn; not to mention Mr. Schulich, Neil, Fred, Lester, Patrick, Josephine, Roe, Susan,

Marty, Leon, Barbara, Meredith, and all the others who had influenced me in my career. I left another piece of my heart that day at Curtis High School . . . .

Chapter IX

Home at Last

Fort Hamilton High School

The afternoon had come. I found myself crossing the Verrazano-Narrows Bridge from my home in Staten Island and getting off at the 92nd Street exit. This route was familiar to me since Charlie and I traveled to Brooklyn at least twice a week to visit relatives, and attend Sunday services at St. Mary's Church. Within a few minutes, I arrived at Fort Hamilton High School and parked my car on the 83rd Street side of the school next to the Bay Ridge landmark called the "Gingerbread House." I was headed for the front of the school which, by design or accident, still looked as though it should have been the back because it faced the athletic field. Getting out of the car, I spotted a well-known figure. Dressed in a suit and tie was Dr. Kriftcher, the BASIS Superintendent. He was waiting to escort me into Fort Hamilton High School. He must have been in a rush because he started to walk briskly to the front entrance while I followed him. My heart was pounding with excitement and joy. I will never forget that day, May 1, 1989. At 3:30 p.m. we passed the steps, walked through the heavy metal entrance doors and entered the school's stately foyer. The quote on the outside wall of the auditorium, and directly in front of us, was so impressive:

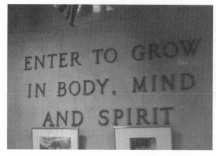 

Inscription mounted on the granite wall in the lobby of
Fort Hamilton High School.
(Photos courtesy Carl Makower, Fort Hamilton High School 2007)

ENTER TO GROW IN BODY, MIND AND SPIRIT. DEPART TO SERVE BETTER YOUR GOD, YOUR COUNTRY AND YOUR FELLOW MAN.

It was thought that this statement was attributed to the first principal, Augustus Ludwig. My research indicated that this was not true. The same quote can be found on the inside wall of Midwood High School, another school built in Brooklyn around the same time as Fort Hamilton. I also know that a similar quote appears on both sides of the 1890 Gate to Harvard Yard, near Widener Library, at Harvard University in Cambridge, Massachusetts. This quote would, nonetheless, remain my theme during my leadership at Fort Hamilton High School, and probably throughout my teaching career.

As Dr. K. and I quickly proceeded down the right ramp of the auditorium, I soon found myself on the stage facing the entire faculty and staff—some 300 people. I was dressed in my new red silk suit, shoulder pads and all. A beautiful metal necklace, which I called "Cleopatra's collar," was draped around my neck. I felt like a queen. I had always wanted to be a math teacher at the school. However, family responsibilities tied me to Staten Island. The only link to Brooklyn was my church, former classmates, and relatives. That was a plus for me. I knew the community, use to live up the block from the school, and was always infatuated with the community that I fell in love with when Dad brought our family from Kentucky to Brooklyn in 1947 and again in 1954.

"Principal Alice" at work in her office at Fort Hamilton High School! *(1991)*

Never in a blue moon would I have dreamt that one day I would be the school's principal. So, here I was once again—back home, not as a math teacher, but as the newly appointed Principal of Fort Hamilton High School. I served from May 1, 1989 until June 30, 1999.

After I was introduced by Dr. K., I stood up in front of everyone. It was a wonderful greeting except for one remark I made during my address. I mistakenly said "Curtis High School" instead of "Fort Hamilton High School." Well, we are all not perfect! I apologized for the slip, but after all, I had just ended eight wonderful years at Curtis. You can't expect me to forget it in one afternoon. Oh well, the slip happened a few more times until I got it perfect—**Fort Hamilton High School**! As soon as I headed towards my office, I couldn't help but notice the broken letter "R" in the word ARISTA—the name of the honor society. It spelt **APISTA**. What was that all about? It seemed to be just another example of the kind of neglect the school had suffered over the decades. That is not how I remembered the school as a student. When I came to the school in 1954, I could not help but remember the pristine condition of the building. I was only fifteen at the time. What a challenge I was facing now. Never say you can't ….never say you can't ….

I entered my office and met the very talented and outstanding school secretary, Barbara Castaldo. She had survived four principals and now she had me. Barbara was my "girl Friday." She was there to help me get acquainted with the school. She greeted me every morning before 7:30 a.m., had coffee ready, and prepared a neatly organized folder filled with my daily mail. She was personable, reliable, and intelligent. She made me laugh. She helped me through the bad days as well as the good days. In plain English, made me feel like a special principal. When she decided ten years later to retire, I followed her. Barbara was a special executive secretary who was a role model for all the other school secretaries in the school. She made my life rewarding and fulfilling for ten years.

Nick Coletto continued to help me at the school until June graduation. He had been an effective acting principal and was always there for me if I needed advice. He left to go to the superintendent's office, and he would ultimately be my superintendent when Dr. K. retired. I wanted to start observing teachers as soon as possible. I inquired about who was one of the best teachers in the building and was told to observe Michael D'Ambrosio. That was an understatement. Upon entering his classroom, unannounced as usual, I found a room of students as intent as possible listening to their teacher. Michael was donned in suit, shirt and tie with a matching handkerchief protruding from his pocket. He was probably one of the most dynamic English teachers I have ever observed. I wished my own English teachers had been like him. He had the students on the edge of their seats as he motivated the lesson. Students were involved in listening, speaking, writing, and thinking skills throughout the lesson. Yes, that day I probably observed one of the best teachers in our city's school system.

I was officially installed as the newly appointed principal on November 6, 1989—a date that I will always remember. When

Mr. Martin Schulich, the principal of Curtis High School, congratulates me at the podium during my official installation ceremony as principal of Fort Hamilton High School. (*November 6, 1989*)

Education officials attending my installation: (L to R) Dr. Noel N. Kriftcher, Superintendent BASIS (Brooklyn and Staten Island Schools); the Honorable James F. Regan, member of the New York City Board of Education; and Herbert Balish, principal of Tottenville High School, and former principal of Port Richmond High School, Staten Island. (*November 6, 1989*)

My mother, Katherine Cury, seated next to Herbert Balish at the dinner following my installation ceremony. *(November 6, 1989)*

In the FHHS girls' gymnasium for a reception following my installation: (L to R) My older brother, George Cury; my mother, Katherine Cury; me; and proud Charlie. *(November, 6 1989)*

Later at the installation dinner: My mother, Katherine Cury, (seated) deep in conversation with Herbert Balish *(R)*. Behind them, standing, my older son, Charles and his soon-to-be wife, Gina Natale. *(November 6, 1989)*

Also at the dinner, *(L to R)*, a side view of Charlie; my second soon-to-be daughter-in-law, Jeanmarie Fallar; and my younger son, Stephen. *(November 6, 1989)*

looking into the audience, I noticed that my son-in-law, Bobby, was seated in the front row but not my pregnant daughter, Cathy. She was expecting the birth of her second child any day, but had insisted she would attend the installation. However, she didn't make it because she was in labor. Bobby called us during the reception to tell us that our second grandchild was born. Mother and baby boy were doing fine. They named our new grandson, Dale Charles.

Seated in the audience at my installation, I also noticed an endearing friend and former mathematics teacher from Prospect Heights, Ruth Trencher. She was seated to the left of me, dressed in a yellow suit and matching hat, but what especially caught my eye was her beautiful smile. I later found out that Ruth was dying of cancer and had insisted that, in spite of her chemotherapy treatments, she was going to share that day with me. She was one of my Orthodox Jewish teachers who was not only wonderful to her students but a gifted mathematician as well. Later on when I attended her shivah (the Jewish ritual of mourning), I ran into the room where all the men were seated so I could express my condolences to her husband. The men were appalled that I didn't know better and gave me some terrible looks. However, her husband stopped them in their tracks and announced to all that, "Mrs. Farkouh has a place next to me for she had my wife's full respect and devotion." Once again, I felt the strength of my upbringing to be a woman of conviction and to love people for what they are and not for whom they are.

As time passed, I got to know all my staff. I will never forget an encounter with one of my social studies teachers, John O'Connor, in the lunchroom. As was common, I liked to eat with the faculty. One day, I was talking to John about Kentucky, when he almost spilled his coffee all over his tray and said in amazement. "You are not *the Alice Cury from Kentucky* whose parents rented our apartment right above us at 7209 Narrows Avenue?" Oh my God, it was *the* O'Connor family! The same family whose apartment we rented and where Willie had pulled that fire alarm on the block when we just moved in, mistakenly taking it for a "giant can opener."

John couldn't stop telling me how nice my family was. He could still recall the breathtaking aromas that seeped through the floors of the two-family house as Mom baked all kinds of Lebanese and Syrian sweets, stuffed grape leaves, kibbee balls, and other Lebanese and Syrian foods. He said our Mom was always giving them a taste of what she made. That was so typical of our nationality. When visitors came, we "opened up the refrigerator and brought everything out" to serve them. Mom was not only trained to cook Middle Eastern foods, but she was also an outstanding southern cook. Lemon meringue, apple, peach, sweet potato, butterscotch, and coconut custard pies made from scratch by her skillful hands were just a few examples of her expertise in southern cooking. She learned to make the "original Kentucky Fried Chicken" using a paper bag filled with flour. Well, I am not going to give away that recipe. Another authentic recipe was one for carrot cake that my Aunt Annie was given back in early 1910 from a European Jew who worked in my Giddi's factory in New York City. The recipe is at least a hundred years old. Mom was an outstanding baker who was known to have the tastiest meals. I still have a magnet in my kitchen which reads, "Katie's Kitchen," and I think she would be happy to know that her recipes have been passed down for three generations already. John O'Connor was so thrilled to meet me. His mother was still alive and he couldn't wait to get home to tell her that Alice, George and Willie had returned . . . .

My first year at Fort Hamilton was rather difficult. The school was undergoing major renovations, totaling almost $41,000,000, of which $11,000,000 was devoted to the building of a state-of-the-art indoor pool complex called a natatorium. The construction costs for the pool amazed me considering that the whole school was completed in 1941 on a budget of around $3,300,000, three times less than this natatorium alone was going to cost now.

I also had to deal with an assistant principal who was not a particularly happy camper when I first arrived. She had been one of the contenders for my job. Fortunately, this tension soon passed because, by the end of the school year, she found a position as principal in a high school outside of New York City. She was a talented educator. I was happy that she got a promotion.

Undoubtedly though, the biggest headache I had to cope with when I started my new job was the construction of the natatorium, and the problem of where to house 900 students while renovations were going on during the school day. The School Construction Authority (SCA) was able to come up with two beautiful prototype classrooms called "modules," but that still left me with the problem of dust, asbestos, lack of space, and upset neighbors.

During the renovation, I was very fortunate to work with an able and gifted civil engineer from the SCA by the name of Hani Arafat (no relation to the Palestinian leader, Yasser Arafat) to supervise the construction. The Egyptian-born Hani supervised the renovation work and the construction of the natatorium. He cared about his work and he did an outstanding job in making sure that the natatorium was constructed as a state-of-the-art facility. Hani made my life a little easier, since I had to deal with the community, surrounding neighbors, and construction activities while school was being conducted as well as a myriad of other concerns in the main building.

Hani was also a confidant. One piece of advice he gave me was when a group of Moslem students came to me on a Friday morning and asked if they could be excused every Friday at noon to go to the mosque and pray. Now, this particular group was not doing well academically and I did not have the same request from my Moslem students who were excelling in school. Since I knew nothing about the Koran, I decided to ask Hani, who was also a Moslem. Hani informed me that the Koran specifically states that when a decision is to be made between education and praying, education comes first. When I brought the students to meet with me, they just giggled and smiled and went back to their classes. It was a good try, but it didn't work.

Believe it or not the UFT worked with me in ensuring that we had the very best conditions not only for the students, but for the faculty and staff as well. The modules would house the students during the renovation. Summer school had to cease and the landscape had to be redesigned because of all the truck traffic on the school grounds. Fort Hamilton High School was always known for the beautiful Magnolia blossom trees that lined the back of the school facing Shore Road. During the construction, a majestic evergreen tree at the back of the school, near the steps, had to be chopped down. What a headache . . . . The neighbors were disappointed to see those "ugly" classroom modules and wanted assurance from me that they would be moved as soon as the renovation was complete. Unfortunately, some neighbors living near the school introduced racial overtones into their opposition to the natatorium. I remember hearing their argument that the new pool was just a way of "Mayor Dinkins' children being bussed to the school." David Dinkins, who was New York City's mayor at the time, was also the city's first African-American to hold that office. The owner of the landmark "Gingerbread House" was totally against the swimming pool being built across his street. He claimed that driving support pillars into the ground was causing massive cracks in his house. I soon lost many of my friends in the neighborhood who were also against the construction of a pool. One dear friend came up to me at the coffee hour in our church and asked, "Shouldn't all that money be spent on education and not swimming?" I immediately reminded her that the swimming pool would be another classroom and that one day someone who learned how to swim could be saving one of her grandchildren.

But as many people as there were who complained to me, there were just as many parents, neighbors, community organizations, and friends who favored and supported me, during this period of time. My superintendent seemed greatly agitated during the building of the pool. However, when it was all over, he was happy. I think he also became happier as the years passed when he saw the changes that were occurring at Fort Hamilton High School. Hani Arafat continued to take me step-by-step through the renovation process so that we were able to work within the framework which had been designed and planned over a decade before I arrived. I would have liked to have had a new auditorium or at least an air-conditioned one, but that wasn't in the plans. However, I was very pleased when New York City Councilman, Vincent Gentile, who represents Bay Ridge and who is also a FHHS graduate from the Class of 1977, managed to secure funding for an air conditioning system for the school auditorium, in 2005, and then in 2007, he succeeded in getting the auditorium's notorious "hard, wooden opera seats" replaced with more comfortable seating!

At the time, the real question running through my mind was, "How in the world was a natatorium approved for the school in the first place?" To answer this, you had to know the individual who "gave birth" to the idea of the swimming pool. It was Tom F. Greene, the high school science teacher, who "fathered" this natatorium. He had been fighting for over two decades to get a pool for the school. I always told Tom that it needed someone like him, who was unrelenting in getting the approval of the Board of Education and the politicians, for the natatorium to become a reality. Tom was not only responsible for getting the funding, but also for supervising the building of the pool; working closely with SCA's engineer, Hani Arafat; planning an aquatics program for our students; and organizing the community use of the pool. At first, I felt the pool should only be used for our students. However, Tom and NYC Councilman, Sal Albanese, of Bay Ridge, soon convinced me of the purpose of the pool. It was not just for the use of the school but also the surrounding community. The pool was, indeed, a big step in winning over the support of the Bay Ridge community.

"Life on Shore Road." This mosaic tile, extending the full length of an upper wall supporting the indoor pool, was especially created for the high school's new Thomas F. Greene Natatorium completed in 1993. *(Photo courtesy Carl Makower Fort Hamilton High School 2007)*

A marvelous mosaic tile mural was designed and crafted within the school to span almost the entire length of one of the pool's upper support walls. It was called, "Life on Shore Road." Figures in the mural included the Greek God, Poseidon, the Canarsie Indians, and the Scandinavian fisherman. It showed scenes from the Dutch and British life, the old 69th Street Staten Island Ferry, and the name, *Water Watch,* written across the bow of a ship crossing the Narrows Bay. A depiction of the building of the Verrazano Bridge and a tugboat moving along the Narrows were also included. I told the local newspapers that we didn't need an expensive statue or monument to dedicate the pool. All we needed was to put the talents of our students to work to create their own lasting tribute to Bay Ridge.

The task of rendering this mosaic mural lay in the hands of Carl Makower, a talented and gifted artist and art teacher at the school, along with our art and science students working with Crystal Siedman, an artist hired by the Board of Education to assist with the school in the restoration of its artworks. It was planned that the mural would not only be embedded in mosaic in the natatorium but would also be depicted in a three-panel oil painting to be hung in the school library. The school's faculty and students offered many ideas about what should be in the mural and all of these were displayed for the entire school to view. The end result of this process was our magnificent mural. "Life on Shore Road," was a replica of ancient, past, present and future life in the Bay Ridge community.

Carl also ensured that the school's older artworks were refurbished and preserved as well. Among them, another mural mounted on the northern corridor of the school's first floor. It was an original from the 1930s produced with government funding by the WPA (Works Progress Administration) which supported artists during the Depression years. The school also had in its possession a book made by another WPA artist, Eli Jacobi. Jacobi was born in Russia, and was saved from homelessness by the WPA who supported his work. By the time he died in 1984, Jacobi was recognized as a significant exponent of the artistic style called Social Realism. The handmade book he gave to the school contained a number of his linoleum prints which he bound by hand with hand-lettered text. In addition, the school possessed a valuable portfolio of black-and-white prints which had been sent out to decorate the walls of schools, like Fort Hamilton, shortly after they opened in the 1930s and 40s.

Thanks to Tom Greene and Carl Makower, the three-panel painting in the library, the mosaic replica in the natatorium, and the school's priceless artworks are now preserved forever and will be a legacy for generations to come.

What was next after the natatorium? I knew that if I could have the community recognize that the school was taking charge of and correcting its problems, perhaps they would look at us in a better light.

Barbara Venito, one of my Assistant Principals of Guidance, was instrumental in helping me to improve the school's image by visiting our feeder schools to praise the virtues of a FHHS

A replica of the natatorium's "Life on Shore Road" mosaic mural was painted in oils and hung in the high school library.
(Photo courtesy Carl Makower Fort Hamilton High School 2007)

This painting was originally given to the school under the federal government's Works Progress Administration (WPA) program in the 1930's to support artists through the Great Depression. The picture was refurbished and preserved during my principalship under the observation of our art teacher, Carl Makower. *(Photo courtesy Carl Makower Fort Hamilton High School 2007)*

education. Barbara was also a graduate of Fort Hamilton High School. Whenever you needed to find a rule or regulation, Barbara had it in her files. She sent cards to the faculty on their birthday, as well as on special holidays. Every year, she hosted a very special dinner at an outside restaurant for her Guidance Department as a way to thank them for all their hard work during the school year.

School spirit was one element of school life that was missing at Fort Hamilton High School. When I arrived in Brooklyn in 1954, my brother and I were shocked that there was no football team and no marching band. Well, that had to be the answer. Let's get a football team! We did. Our first football team came to fruition in 1991. This was accomplished by Joe Pancila, who helped with fundraising; Herb Solomon, the Assistant Principal of Health and Physical Education; and, most of all, the newly-selected football coach, Vincent Laino (known to all of us as Vinnie). They were all instrumental in helping me put the pieces of the puzzle together to form the FHHS FOOTBALL TIGERS. I will never forget the day when Herb brought Vinnie into my office to be interviewed for the head coach position. I took Herb on the side and said, "This young man wants to be a football coach? Look at his size." Herb smiled at me and said, "Alice, don't judge a book by its cover." That was an understatement. Vinnie had been trained by Moe Finklestein, a legendary local high school football coach, who trained the Thomas Jefferson High School teams for many years. In Vinnie, you could not ask for a more caring and dedicated football coach. He took the Tigers in hand, trained them, taught them values and ethics, expected them to keep up with their academics, and was a role model for his students and football players. When the team participated in an assembly, they would walk into the auditorium dressed in suits and ties. When a member did not follow his tutelage, they were out. He trained them to be physically fit, as well as to be excellent football players. Within two years, our football team (Varsity B) won the City Championships for the Public School Athletic League (PSAL).

FHHS Football Varsity Division B won two consecutive city-wide PSAL Division B championships and was placed in Division A in 1994 with a cumulative record of 25-0 by mid-October 1994. Football coach, Vincent Laino, is standing in the third row, 5th from left. The young boy standing in front of Vincent is his son, Frank. *(Photo courtesy Vinnie Laino 1997)*

Vinnie's Varsity B Team became a Varsity A Team and has continued to do quite well. What do you mean quite well? On December 3, 2005 and December 2, 2006, the Football Tigers won the PSAL Varsity A Football City Championship title for all New York City. What a proud day for the Varsity Football Team! What a proud day for Fort Hamilton High School! Vinnie's work ethic was exemplary. He was also training future prospective coaches just as his mentor, Moe Finklestein, did for him. Vinnie's lovely wife, Lisa, and their two sons, had been actively involved in the life of the school, and Vinnie had managed to build a strong Football Parents Association. Yes, Herb, I agree. Don't judge a book by its cover.

What was next after a football team, and a state-of-the-art natatorium? Well, of course, students had to be allowed to play music in the cafeteria, and had Friday ethnic dances during the lunch periods. Their dances were well run and supervised. Clubs sold their food and young people danced. I even danced with them. I learned the Salsa, Greek dances, and perfected my Arabic dances as well. So, I started to focus my attention on the Music Department. That was some challenge. I turned to a good friend and colleague of mine through the years, Larry Laurenzano. He had been my Stephen's private drum tutor in fifth grade. I believe these lessons raised Stephen's self-esteem so much that he later graduated third in his class in 1983 at Curtis High School. Larry was just the kind of inspiring musician we needed at FHHS—and he became my new Assistant Principal of Music.

The Music Department exploded with Larry on board. I was very fortunate to attract him to our school. You could think of Larry as the "Pied Piper of Staten Island." When he ran a music program, the youth picked up their instruments and followed him. Yes, the "Pied Piper of Staten Island" came to Brooklyn. I will never forget the 1991 graduation ceremony which was the third under my principalship, but the first one at the school for Larry. At the end of the ceremony, the graduates threw their caps into the air. One landed in the orchestra pit. As Larry was conducting, he felt a tap on his shoulder. Baton in hand, he turned his head and saw a student pointing to his cap on the floor next to Larry. I thought Larry was either going to have a heart attack or smack the "impolite graduate" with his baton. At the end of the graduation ceremony, Larry came up to me and apologized for the unruly behavior of many of the graduates. He told me in his soft but firm voice, "That will never happen again." And it didn't. Every graduation ceremony from then on was conducted in an orderly and eloquent manner. Larry and I chuckled from time to time whenever I reminded him of that incident.

The first auditorium presentation from the Symphonic Band was the Latino song, "La Bamba." The Latino students in the audience went crazy! Up until then, they felt that no one at the school had ever recognized their culture. Since our student population was thirty-eight per cent Latino, it was about time! Larry knew how to win over the students with music. You never heard

Larry call a male student "boy." It was always, "son." Yes, students were indeed his children. Today, the auditorium is dedicated to him with a magnificent plaque outside its doors, **The Laurence Laurenzano Theater**. Grief hit the school when Larry took deathly sick and passed away in 2005. The music world lost a great champion, but his memory lives on in all the young people and educators who were touched by Larry Laurenzano.

Our COSAs made sure that we continued the heritage of Friday night dances to raise money. The only changes I made were that there could not be "very dim lights," "smoking machines," and uninvited "guests" to the dances. In addition, I was able to get permission from the superintendent's office to set up cameras in the hallways and cafeteria to make sure that the students did not violate any school safety rules. If something got stolen, broken, or an intruder entered, we would eventually find out who the culprit was. This was my way of making the school safe, and at the same time, supervising functions. Gates were installed to close off areas on the first floor so that school safety officers and faculty members could secure the area during weekday school functions, as well as on the weekends and holidays.

One major concern that I addressed was the removal of graffiti on school grounds, and in the Bay Ridge community. What better way to stop the "graffiti artists" than to take a picture of the "tag" (the signature of the graffiti artist), and share it with the faculty and staff, as well as the local police at the 68th Police Precinct. Neighbors would constantly call me up to have me identify a "graffiti artist." I would take my photograph books and go out with my deans or assistant principal, Mike, to identify the tag. It would be a matter of an hour, a day, or maybe a week, but we would catch the offender. The best punishment was to have the student responsible clean up the damage, and pay for the materials to cover up the problem. The question is, why graffiti in the first place? Sometimes it was for the fun of it, but the majority of times, it was because the young man—and it usually was a young man—was crying out for help.   I remember one particular incident where a student (let us call him J) wrote "f— you" on a desk in a classroom. We knew who the student was and had his mother come in to discuss the matter, and pay $250 to clean up the desk. His mother was absolutely furious! "My son did not do this and I am not going to pay $250!" she adamantly stated. J turned to his mother and said, "Yes, I did it." The mother was so embarrassed that she couldn't wait to write out a check for $250. Why did he want to embarrass his mother? Why did he do this? Unfortunately, it would be left to the school's guidance counselor to help him with the problem which his mother didn't think he had. That was the saddest part of this incident. His mother had no clue as to what was bothering him.

I continued to get support from Mike and the dean's office. Mike, as well as deans such as Al, Martha, Barbara, Mike, Walter, Bob, and others would be in and outside of the school's perimeter making sure that the school was safe and that outsiders, who were usually truants from other schools in Brooklyn, knew that Fort Hamilton High School was not a place to visit during school hours. Many students called Mike "Robot Cop." I did not like this nickname because I didn't think Mike acted like that at all . Mike was as real as the day was long. He continued to serve the school in such an outstanding manner that he and the Dean's Office were instrumental in moving Fort Hamilton High School into the forefront of BASIS schools: BASIS included many of the Brooklyn high schools and all the Staten Island high schools. Deputy Assistant Superintendent, Dr. Judy Curran, put it very nicely when she described Fort Hamilton High School as **"a Gem of BASIS."**

There were so many memorable incidents involving students from the school. Can you imagine that at one of the principal's suspension hearings we discovered—and so did a student—that his "mother" was really his grandmother, and his "aunt" was really his mother. Although I will never know the reasons for the mother's decision to be known as her son's "aunt", I was very saddened that day for all involved. I wondered if the boy had ever felt deep down that his grandmother wasn't really his "mother"? I can't say, but what do you think?

Well, it was obvious to me that more had to be done about school spirit and having the students bond with the school, regardless of what baggage they brought with them when they first arrived. We had divided the school population, which was close to 4,000 students, into houses where each house constituted a theme: Honors Academy House, Careers House, Fine Arts and Performing Arts House, among others. Larry, along with his capable assistant, Mahasin, established the first Marching Regiment. Decked out in uniforms, the FHHS Marching Regiment, became renowned not only in the community of Bay Ridge, but throughout the city, state, and nation.

One new program that local community members, and FHHS graduates, such as Larry Morrish, helped me to establish was the Junior Reserve Officers Training Corps (JROTC) Program for young men and women. The Army JROTC students were interested in a leadership program, and perhaps going into college with a scholarship or entering the services. They accomplished all of these goals and more. Larry Laurenzano took over the supervision of not only the Music Department but also the Army JROTC program, the Business Department, and the Fine Arts Department. The different hats he wore earned him the right to have a full-time paraprofessional assistant. As a result, I transferred Janet General to be Larry's assistant. The teacher-in-charge of the JROTC Program at school was a retired army officer, Lt. Colonel Lee Anderson, who was not only an outstanding educator, administrator, and supervisor, but a wonderful role model for our students. The after-school Aquatics Program, supervised by Tom Greene, was another program which began to attract local community students to our school. Since the Honors Academy had higher requirements to get into, and to stay in the program, an Honors Academy Program placement test was set up. Fort Hamilton High School was no longer considered "the last resort to go to if you couldn't get into any other school."

The house coordinators, paras, school aides, and guidance department personnel helped to reach out to excessively absent students. The paras would go to the homes of truants five days-a-week and send them back to school during the day. It was not unusual for paras such as Charlene, Mohamed Shohatee, and Lorraine to go to the park, restaurants, luncheonettes, or billiard halls to literally "drag" absent students back to school.

Joanne, and her sister, Cathy, along with Norma, Lorraine, Barbara Castaldo, Barbara Golia, Gene, Irene, Elsa, Helen, Joanne, Bob L., Joyce, Adele, Helen, Lenore, Marie, Pat, Janet, Sue, Wendy, Carol, Rose, Debbie, Harold, Laila, and Jim were among the team of secretaries, school aides, and paras who helped us improve the quality of life at FHHS for both students and personnel. The Program Office became efficient and functional under the leadership of Steve Satin, Joe Guinta, Susan, and Carol. Grade advisors, and Guidance Counselors, like Jo Ann Porto, were the best in the city. Test Coordinator, and talented mathematics teacher, Lenore Satin, and her school aide, Marie, were fantastic at their job. They tracked students who needed the appropriate Regents and RCT's.

I couldn't forget the great custodial staff starting with our custodian, Tom, as well as custodial staff members, Kevin and Mario.

The newly-appointed Assistant Principal of Security, Mike Kozlowski, and Dean's Office personnel tightened up security both inside and outside the school, as well as its borders. Neighbors started to trust us once again. I would listen to their concerns and then, when appropriate, solve the problems. I used to get on the public address system and say, "Now hear this." Just joking. I would get on the public address system, and remind students that they were "ambassadors of our school." I would remind them that if they did anything inappropriate on the way to school or going home, I would give them a principal's or superintendent's suspension. Inappropriate behavior included fighting, throwing ketchup outside the windows of a bus on the way home, writing graffiti on public or private property, etc. It worked. It took a while, but it worked.

I think the main reason for the reduction of inappropriate behavior was the fact that Fort Hamilton High School was becoming a "school of choice." The view of the Narrows Bay gave the school a sense of peacefulness in a time of problems. School spirit was on the rise. Here again, I was helped by the talents of another of the school's assistant principals, Susan Russo, my able and caring Assistant Principal of Physical and Health Education. She, along with her department, started to change the typical physical education offerings so as to better encourage student interest. A variety of physical education classes were offered, as opposed to the typical gym classes of the past.

We fought a long time for a scoreboard for the Fort Hamilton athletic field. The problem was that the field was not officially school property. It belonged to the Parks Department. Eventually, we managed to get a scoreboard to use for our school team games, but we had to keep it on our property behind a metal chain fence. That was okay. We could deal with that. We just wanted that scoreboard and we got it.

Various career programs were created or improved: the Culinary Arts Institute, with a state-of-the-art commercial kitchen, the Health Careers Room; the Law Institute, which was set up to duplicate a courtroom; and the Computer Technology Room, with state-of-the-art technology. Larry was able to design his own music suite, and increase his music offerings, such as a Junior Concert Band, and Symphonic Orchestra.

Many individuals improved the school. The Fort Hamilton High School Natatorium was dedicated to Thomas F. Greene, and the FHHS Alumni Association donated a magnificent plaque which was mounted outside the pool to honor him. The Law Classroom was dedicated to Judge Chris (Christopher J.) Mega, alumnus from the Class of 1949, a former New York state senator, and at the time a presiding judge for New York State's Court of Claims. The Computer Technology classroom was dedicated to

New York City Councilman, Sal Albanese, in recognition of his unrelenting commitment to helping the school, particularly during the fight with the school's neighbors to get the natatorium financed and built.

Howard Brenner, the Assistant Principal of Mathematics and Computer Science, performed his job so well that the school's achievement levels in mathematics were parallel with those of Stuyvesant High School, a highly-competitive math and science specialty school within NYC's public education system whose test scores matched its reputation for academic excellence. Steve Wolfson was the Assistant Principal of Social Studies and the Law Institute. He was my confidant and supervisor-in-charge in the event of my absence. Tobias Weissman was one of the most able Assistant Principals of Special Education the city has ever had. He worked closely with BASIS and made sure the school was in compliance with city, state, and federal mandates for students with disabilities. Tobias was also a talented artist and taught ceramics to the regular students, as well as to the special education students. He was instrumental in the design of two ceramic tile walls, the *Welcome Wall* representing almost fifty different languages, and the *Respect Wall* depicting seventeen different languages. The beautiful *Welcome Wall* is made out of fifty carved blocks joined together on a large plaque that now hangs in the administrative hallway adjacent to the school's main lobby. Bronze-colored streaks flowed from block-to-block uniting the languages. The word "Welcome" is spelled out in each language, including sign language for the deaf. Tobias made sure that the word for welcome, in Arabic, would be in the center to welcome me to the school. One language that was left out was Norwegian. Unfortunately, no one told Tobias that, in the 1940s and 1950s, Norwegian immigrants and residents were predominant in Bay Ridge, and therefore in the school as well. The famous "Norwegian Parade" is still celebrated in Bay Ridge. Well, maybe one day an addendum will be placed to honor the first and largest group of students who came to FHHS. A replica of the *Welcome Wall*

The *"Welcome Wall"* (1991) was created by FHHS special education students under the guidance of our ceramics teacher and Assistant Principal, Tobias Weissman. The mural's ceramic tiles depict the word "Welcome" in different languages. *(Photo courtesy Carl Makower Fort Hamilton High School 2007)*

plaque was made for the Ocean Terrace building in Staten Island which houses the former BASIS office (now known as the Regional Center of ISC— Integrated Service Center). Thanks to Tobias Weissman, our school will always be remembered there. Our students did the work, of course. Yet, this is still a beautiful link between Staten Island and Brooklyn for generations to enjoy. It was a fact that, during my tenure at Fort Hamilton High School, the student population came from over fifty countries, mirroring NYC's real ethnic melting pot. Tobias's leadership and dedication were also reflected in the love and devotion he gave to students with special needs. The second *Respect Wall* plaque was created by Tobias, and his ceramic students, to promote and encourage harmony and love for each other regardless of race, color, creed, or language. Tobias will always be very special to me; as will be the Assistant Principal of Science, Carl Raab; followed by Assistant Principal of Science, Tom Greene, because together they built a strong and well-respected Science Department.

The *"Respect Wall" (1996)* was another artistic project created by special
education students under the direction FHHS Assistant Principal, Tobias
Weissman. In this mural, ceramic tiles display the word "respect" in 17 different
languages, including the concept, "Respect: To get it, you have to give it."
(Photo courtesy Carl Makower Fort Hamilton High School 2007)

Another of my special friends at the school was David
Whitebook. What can I say about David, whom I nicknamed,
"Mr. Fort Hamilton High School."

When I arrived, David was a COSA (Coordinator of Student
Affairs). However, it was only a matter of time before I would select him as the Assistant Principal of Organization. Jack
Fakterowitz, who was my Assistant Principal of Organization,
befriended me and helped me through the first two years of my
principalship. However, Jack retired in June 1991 and David took
over the following month. Before Jack left, he trained David so
that there would be a smooth transition. That was what was very
special about Jack. He cared about the school and was always
there to help even after he left. That is what real leadership is all
about. Jack was special to the school and very special to me.

As for David, he was not only an outstanding mathematics
teacher, and colleague, but he was devoted to the school and its
students. He played an important role in improving the image of

Charlie and me, in my doctoral robes, following the graduation ceremony
to receive my Doctorate in Educational Administration from Teachers College,
Columbia University, New York. *(May 20, 1991)*

FHHS, building up its alumni association, and bonding the community of Bay Ridge with the high school.

Sandi Mummolo was a personal friend, as well as the school's talented and able Assistant Principal of English. She, with the help of dedicated teachers such as Mike, Carol, Bill, and others, did a fine job improving the different programs in the English Department. Judi Haliou was one of the best Assistant Principals of Foreign Languages and ESL (English As A Second Language) in the city. She and her department teachers, paras, and aides worked very hard in helping immigrants, as well as American-born students, improve their language skills. FHHS soon offered seven foreign languages: Arabic, Chinese, French, Greek, Italian, Spanish, and Russian. Latin was restored to the curriculum. With the impetus and push from teachers like Janet, Helena, Florence, Doris, Lisa, Aratif, Christine, and Argyri, as well as David Whitebook, ESL students were allowed to be selected into the National Honors Society (formerly called ARISTA). I am **forever grateful** to wonderful and devoted teachers and assistant principals who helped to turn our school around. Yes, "it takes a whole village to educate a child."

Two years into my tenure at Fort Hamilton High School, I passed a milestone in my professional career when I received my Doctorate in Education. On May 20, 1991, my family attended my graduation from Teachers College at a ceremony on the beautiful Columbia University campus in New York City. It was on this day that I received my Doctoral Degree in Educational Administration. I had written a dissertation, *School of Membership and Academic Engagement: Formative Case Study at Sunset Hill High School.* My hypothesis was that if the impediments to learning and school memberships were lowered, then a student would succeed no matter what baggage he or she brought to school. I used this theory to create an atmosphere of learning at Fort Hamilton High School. This atmosphere led to generating school spirit and academic achievement throughout the life of many students at the school. One very important factor in the school's growing success was that it was not an *I* or a *Me*, but a *We*. We—the administrators, teachers, staff, students, and parents—started to buy into the life of the school. Among the parents—Nydia Santiago, John Vazquez, Maria Makrinos, Sandy Bernhard, Immacolata Pellegrino, and Linda Varacalli were instrumental in helping us to produce a school of excellence.

Well, things were moving at the Fort. What was next? What else, but the academics. In researching why our students were not earning enough Regents-Endorsed diplomas, I soon discovered that not only were they not being encouraged, but it wasn't a priority of the school. Well, that changed. It took time and patience but the entire school bought into the goal that academic standards needed to be raised, starting with the Guidance Department, under the supervision of Barbara, and later on Margaret Lacey-Berman, who took Barbara's place after she retired; the PTA; Pete Devlin, our newly-appointed COSA; and David, our Assistant Principal of Organization. We also received invaluable support from the Student Government under the leadership of Vanessa Mercurio, a bright and caring student leader. As the years unfolded, our Regents-Endorsed diplomas increased. Margaret Lacey-Berman continued to be supportive of our goal. She started off as a Physical and Health Education teacher, became Senior Advisor, and then the Assistant Principal of Guidance and Support Services. She was a hard worker and knew what to do when it came to promoting the Houses and improving the number of Regents-Endorsed Diplomas. Even Larry Laurenzano reviewed the music, arts and business three and five-year offerings to encourage students to pursue accreditation for a Regents-Endorsed diploma in these disciplines. As time passed, student achievement, as well as student attendance, was on the rise.

Fort Hamilton High School continued to improve. However, along with success came difficulty. Enrollment soared. There were no more spaces available to accommodate extra students. Some parents resorted to any means to get their children into the school. So addresses had to be checked and home visits had to be made. We even had to go back to the intermediate school records to see if there were false addresses used by parents to get their children into the school. On the positive side, I was happy to see Fort Hamilton High School's reputation being restored to what it was in the '40s,'50s, and '60s. Who was responsible? Not one person, but an entire family made up of the leadership, students, and parents. School spirit, coupled with the improvement in academics and course offerings, helped to bring about the change. When I came upon a card that I had saved for many years, I was surprised to find that it was from my Mr. Balish. It was a thank you card for inviting him to visit Fort Hamilton High School. One particular quote from the card exemplified the insight and vision of Herbert Balish. He was thrilled at the many wonderful things he had seen on his tour of the school. His last line was: "**Guard it. A Public School in a Private School Setting. But there are so many wonderful touches.**" He underlined the phrase "so many wonderful." His friendship, vision, and nurturing attitude towards me during the decades culminated in these words. God bless you, Mr. Balish, wherever you are. I expect that he is looking down at all of us who were touched by his leadership, love, and devotion to excellence in education.

I know that our Superintendent, Dr. K., followed by Superintendent Nick Coletto, were pleased as well. Yes, Nick Coletto had been the acting principal at FHHS prior to my arrival in 1989. Now, he was our superintendent. He was so pleased with the school that he decided to teach a New York State Anatomy class to our brightest science students early in the morning regardless of his busy day as school superintendent.

I got involved in representing my union (CSA) during negotiations with the teachers union on Circular 6R. What a disaster. In my opinion, the Board of Education gave away the store by agreeing to the particulars of Circular 6R which had the end result of taking more teachers out of their compensatory jobs and replacing them with school aides. I will never forget at one point in the discussions when the head of the teachers union (in front of UFT members) told my superintendent to "Go f— himself." As usual, Superintendent Nick Coletto did not lose his cool, but answered in a polite tone, "Biologically, that is an impossibility." The UFT leader apologized to him after lunch, but she had made a point. It was obvious that the entire executive board knew the power of the teachers' union to demean the superintendent of BASIS. Times are changing today, and the mayor of New York City is holding strong in trying to make changes within the political climate. Will it work? Time will tell.

I had applied for a Deputy Superintendent's position for BASIS in the late winter of 1998. Dr. Margaret Harrington, a personal friend and colleague who went back in my career to Curtis High School, did not select me. She never said it, but we knew it was not her policy to select someone from the same superintendency. Maybe she was right. However, this changed my entire future. Instead, she offered me a SUR (Schools Under Review) position. Two of my other colleagues decided not to take this offer unless it was pensionable. Dr. Harrington felt the city's mayor at the time would never make it pensionable. So I was surprised when one of my colleagues took the job after I thought we had all mutually agreed not to take it because of the pension issue. In a few months, the position not only became pensionable but that individual became a deputy superintendent. Oh well, that was the way the ball bounced. One thing our family taught us was to be loyal to our word. That was a very important issue with Dad and Mom, and that was the way I wanted it as well.

I had decided to retire if I got a job in New Jersey as a superintendent or a job in the private sector. I was too young to stop working fulltime. I felt I had so much to offer. By chance, I saw an advertisement in the *New York Times* about Poly Prep Country Day School in Dyker Heights, Brooklyn, having an opening as Head of the Upper School. I applied and was selected. I was to start July 1, 1999. I was thrilled. Even though I felt sad leaving my school after ten years, I truly felt at the time that the Board of Education did not want experienced and qualified educators. It was apparent that "the old way was the best way." When an individual actually exhibits the turning around of a school, the improvement of attendance and achievement, and the creation of a school setting which nurtured our youth, then that individual should be promoted. Wouldn't you think so?

June 30, 1999 was my last day at Fort Hamilton High School. I had packed all my belongings, pictures, books, important and personal documents. Around 3:00 p.m., there was a commotion in the back of the school. I decided to go see what the problem was. It was summer school registration and students from other schools were impatient. They didn't want to go to summer school, no less waste time during the registration. They wanted to get in and out fast. I walked out the back entrance and addressed the crowd. They asked, "Who is that lady?" Someone answered, "You don't know who she is? That's our principal. You better be quiet." Within a few seconds, I quieted down the group and informed them that if they had any intentions of coming into my school, they'd better be respectful. Within a moment, the words still on my lips, quietness came into the air. Later on, Officer Courtney Grant, the New York City police officer stationed at the school, came to my office to say good-bye and wish me well. He was a little puzzled and said, "It's your last few hours here and you still care about the school?" I told Officer Grant that there will always be people who will care about the school for the school is on a solid foundation. I still wonder why I left. Another book could be written about that. I may have become a deputy superintendent in four months; I may have continued up the career ladder that year. But it was not to happen for I had made my decision to retire from the New York City Board of Education, currently called the Department of Education. What is sad is the fact that I had, and still have, so much to offer the system, but it was time to move on, Alice. Time to touch the hearts of others. I hoped that I would.

Chapter X

Schools of the Privileged

I retired from the New York City Board of Education on June 30, 1999. It was obvious that Mayor Rudolph W. Giuliani was not ready to give the principals a raise at the time. If you were a high school principal with a student population of 600 or 4,200, as I was, you still got the same salary. So, I decided to apply outside the system. I was very lucky that Headmaster Bill Williams of Poly Prep Country Day School was interested in hiring me as the first female Head of the Upper School. It was a pleasure and an honor to be selected by him. He was a gentleman who was humble, kind, and most of all caring for the school, as well as the students. He had put his heart into the school for over three decades and earned the respect of every graduating class. It was Headmaster Bill Williams who was able to raise the status of the school, not only academically, but financially. His Board of Trustees respected his opinion. His students from former graduating classes would constantly visit him. Most of all, he was respectful to me. He realized that I was a product of the public school system and not the independent schools. My reputation preceded me and he wanted me to become part of his faculty. The first year was rather "rough" for me, but Bill Williams was supportive of my leadership, and gave me the confidence I needed to go on the next year. Unfortunately, my relationship with one of the principal's assistants soured to the point where I found him to be very hostile towards me. I was sad about this because he was a talented educator. Anyway, Headmaster Bill Williams retired in June, 2000, and I thought I had the support of his replacement. I had learned from the problems I experienced in my first year, as I was learning the ropes of administering at a school for the privileged. So imagine my surprise when the new headmaster asked me to leave at the end of the school year. He told me that, "it was the hardest thing he had to do," but he did it. The administrator, with whom I had had those run-ins, was also leaving because he had been promoted to headmaster at a school in another state. I will never forget being told by the new headmaster that he had been informed that I had taken my position at the school on the understanding that I "only took the job for two years." So sad for them and so sad for me....but never say you can't ....never say you can't.

Even though I was told in December that I had to leave at the end of the school year, I intended to hold my head up high, and continue working for parents, students, and faculty in my capacity as Head of the Upper School—and I did. I continued to perform my responsibilities, and put my heart into the job as I have always done. One of my deans once told me, "You are some gutsy lady." Yes, I was. I was brought up to respect others, hold your head high, and perform your responsibilities no matter how difficult the road ahead. I did. The faculty gave me a farewell party and over forty "invited guests" attended. My deans also gave me a farewell luncheon. One of my favorites, and the most respected dean in the school, whispered in my ear that if the entire faculty had been invited to my farewell party, everyone would have attended.

I felt good about that remark because I loved Poly Prep during my short stay, and I am still in contact with faculty and staff, former students and their parents, as well as retirees. I served two memorable roles at Poly Prep–first, as Head of the Upper School and second, as a master teacher. I loved every minute that I spent there teaching. Yes, the schools for the privileged are different from public schools, and I believe that what I learned during that short period should have been shared with the top leaders of our public schools. We can learn a lot from the many programs of Poly Prep Country Day School. Thank you, Headmaster Bill Williams, for giving me the privilege to work at Poly and learn from my experiences. Poly Prep Country Day School is a wonderful place to get an excellent education in a private setting. I will always remember my endearing friends, particularly Carol, Marie, Susan, Ralph, John R., and Dorothy. Their smiles and laughter brightened up my life in that short period, and I will be forever grateful for their true friendship.

Before I left Poly Prep, I had many offers to join the faculty of other schools. A Moslem school had asked me to join the top leadership. I offered to help them, but not become the head of the school. When I found out that I would have to dress like a Moslem female and cover my head, forget that! I tried to explain to members of the Board that I was a Christian. My priest, my husband, and my children would be furious if I would have agreed to take it. The director of a graduate program at the College of Staten Island offered me an outstanding position. I was ready to take it but there was no written agreement that I would have a waiver to protect my pension, so I decided against it.

Another school for the privileged, Adelphi Academy in Bay Ridge, approached me to become their new headmistress. At one time, the school was renowned. It was the first coeducational independent school to open its doors in the late nineteenth century. After a great deal of fiscal difficulties in the first half of the twentieth century, the school trustees sold their original building in downtown Brooklyn and bought the Kallman Home on 86th Street and Ridge Boulevard in Bay Ridge. After some encouragement from my personal friend, John Abi-Habib, and a few members of the Board of Trustees, I decided to take their offer. For the first six months, I loved my job. I called many of my contacts from other Independent Schools and slowly started to build a sound, educational program for the school. I also taught a class at Adelphi, and since the headmistress is also the master teacher, I decided to teach the Advanced Placement Calculus Class. One of my initiatives at the school was to introduce Advanced Placement classes in Biology, English, Art, and Mathematics. The Board of Trustees was extremely supportive of me. The President of the Board, as well as her mother, who was also a board member, were always there for me. It was unfortunate that personal circumstances prevented me from running the school effectively. I resigned. That is a great word—resign. I was moving on.

Chapter XI

What is Higher Education all about?

soon found myself hired by the Mathematics Department of The College of Staten Island (CSI) as an Adjunct Assistant Professor. I had earned two masters degrees at the former Richmond College (now part of the College of Staten Island), and was placed in the Alumni Hall of Fame at the college in 1997. Home again. It was now time to leave the schools for the privileged and return to the classroom.

I was interviewed by a very talented group of educators from the Mathematics Department during the summer of 2002. They informed me that they were most impressed by my resumé, and wanted to know if I was interested in becoming a part-time member of the department. I was very impressed by their attitude towards me, and how they were interested in hiring a qualified teacher for their students. I told them I couldn't earn too high a salary because, as a retiree, I was limited in what I could earn from the city. They laughed because it was unusual to hire someone who didn't want a higher salary. I said yes, and soon found myself teaching two Algebra and Trigonometry classes during the fall semester of 2002. The professional staff in the Mathematics Department was very supportive. I loved teaching and seeing students learn. My goal was to engage students, have them responsible for doing their homework, and tutor them before, during, and after my specific tutorial hour once a week. Seeing students learn has been my goal throughout my career.

Life there was invigorating as an educator. Dr. Marlene Springer had arrived in 1994 as the newly-appointed president of the school. As an outstanding leader, she took the school and turned it around. Some say it was because of the campus, while others say that it was getting better before she arrived. You can take a beautiful location and still fail. Was it better before she arrived? I can only answer this through my experience as an Assistant Principal of Mathematics at Curtis High School (1981-1989), and Principal of Fort Hamilton High School (1989-1999). No, it wasn't doing well before her arrival. She brought many innovative programs to the school, including an Honors Program.

At CSI, I caught up once again with an old friend from over the years, Angelo Aponte, who was now the college's First Vice President for Finance and Administration. We had worked alongside each other at Port Richmond High School, Prospect Heights High School, Curtis High School and now CSI. He was busy working on a dream of his to bring student housing to the campus. Good Luck, Angelo. If anyone can do it, you sure can.

At the College of Staten Island, I also had the opportunity to interact with talented colleagues, both part-time as well as full-time members. I was fortunate to get elected to the University Faculty Senate from 2004-2006. When I started out at CSI, I had been reluctant to teach students in the math remediation program, known as Math 020. After my first semester of teaching them, I swore I would never do it again. Well, I had no choice, and I had to teach the course again. When the placement test for mathematics changed from a less challenging test called CMAT to the more complex COMPASS test, I started to have a different attitude about the course. Students were so needy for good teaching and being successful. They made me feel needed. So three semesters later, I was still teaching a Math 020 class. It was hard to get them out of the room at the end of the period because they were so focused on passing the remediation class and in particular, the college proficiency exam. Isn't it wonderful to be appreciated? What about my other classes at CSI? I taught a variety of mathematics classes ranging from remediation courses, through calculus. I even enjoyed teaching mathematics classes for future elementary teachers. Whatever level of mathematics, I tried to make mathematics fun. Students laugh when I say that, but they also add that they can see it in my face that I love mathematics. That's what it's all about. I remember once attending a ceremony at the New York Public Library in Manhattan during my time as principal of FHHS. I had to bring our school's June valedictorian with me. The guest speaker said something very poignant which summarized my own feeling about teaching and learning. He told the valedictorians assembled there from every public high school in the city that when you have a passion for something you really enjoy doing, then you will always be successful in life. My passion is teaching and then carrying this to another level by helping educators convey this passion to their students. Teachers, administrators, as well as young people, are our students. To be successful, you must love what you are doing, and then bring this love into the heart and soul of those around you. I continued to teach in the Mathematics Department at The College of Staten Island as an Assistant Adjunct Professor until January 2008. My main aspiration was to open the eyes of my students to the joys of learning mathematics. I hope I accomplished this goal.

Chapter XII

Final Chapter

I now have the time to concentrate on my family, as I begin the end of my career in education. God has blessed Charlie and me with not only three beautiful children–Cathy, Charles, and Stephen; as well as their spouses, Robert, Gina, and Jeanmarie; but with seven loving grandchildren. They are Tyler, Dale, Stephen, Matthew, Christopher, Nicole, and Jessica. It was unfortunate that both my father and Charlie's passed away early in our children's lives. However, our children have profound memories of their two grandmothers.

We try to remind our children of their heritage, and to let them know that their heritage is never to be forgotten. Our grandparents arrived in America from Lebanon and Syria to escape the tyranny of other dictatorships. That was what their purpose in coming to America was all about. No matter what our nationality, the most important thing to remember is our roots, teaching our children basic values, and never giving up our passions for what we truly believe in. Never to say, "I can't do it." These words are not in my vocabulary. From the 1700s to the present, our family history has played a dominant part in our legacy. We have been nurtured throughout the generations to respect and love those around us without prejudice or hate. If only

The Pride of Our Life—Our children (L to R) Stephen Charles, Catherine Marie, and Charles George. This picture was taken on the day of Charles and Gina's wedding, August 2, 1991.

our world could listen to the winds of our universe, and breathe in this air of peace and freedom which has sustained my own family. If people of all denominations and races could do the same, then there would be no need for wars, for anger among our neighbors, and hatred for mankind. Smell the roses, remember God's love for us—and perhaps we can set an example for future generations. Our world has lasted for over four billion years, and I know that we will sustain future life on this beautiful planet called Earth.

I have not forgotten Fort Hamilton High School and continue to be supportive through the school alumni association. In November 1991, an alumni "Hall of Fame" was introduced to recognize former graduates who had made their mark in their communities or careers. As present-day students walk the school's third floor corridor outside the library, they can read the plaques of past graduates who have been honored for their success in medicine, athletics, education, art, music, politics, journalism, and business. This Hall of Fame is the *Pride of the Graduates*. I

Charlie and I met in February, were engaged in May, and got married in September of 1960. Now, as we approach our Golden Jubilee Wedding Anniversary in 2010, we are just as in love as the day when we first took our marriage vows. We are proud of our three children—Catherine, Charles, and Stephen, and our seven grandchildren—Tyler, Dale, Stephen, Christopher, Matthew, Nicole, and Jessica. God has blessed us!

I leave this book as a testimony for our children, and grandchildren, and their future generations. They will have a record of our past, and present for the future. Lead, know thyself, inspire, and

Never Say You Can't...Never Say You Can't...

was honored that my late bother, George, and myself, were among the first inductees to the Hall of Fame. At present, I am the president of the Fort Hamilton High School Alumni Association , as well as the editor of the alumni newsletter. Charlie, a Class of 1949 FHHS graduate, is a former president of the alumni association, and now serves as an officer and member on the executive board. It was Charlie who introduced the newsletter during his presidency. Sixteen issues later, Fort Hamilton alum still enjoy reading the bi-yearly publication! Alum from all parts of the

OFFICE OF THE PRESIDENT

BOROUGH OF BROOKLYN
CITY OF NEW YORK

Citation

*W*hereas, Brooklyn is home to a large and vibrant Lebanese population giving us proud claim to the title "Lebanese Capital of the USA," and our Lebanese residents add so much to the rich tapestry of cultural, ethnic, and religious diversity for which Brooklyn is known – as followers of Islam, Christianity, and Judaism – it is only fitting that we join our residents of Lebanese origin or descent and pay tribute to their extraordinary culture; and

*W*hereas, Brooklyn welcomes our residents, friends, and visitors of Lebanese descent – and those who wish they were – to the Annual Lebanese Heritage Reception to pay tribute to Lebanese Heritage Month, to take note of the outstanding contributions that our residents of Lebanese descent have made to our quality of life – from the gustatory pleasures of kibbeh, Lebanese coffee and arak, to contributions in the arts from the likes of poet Kalil Gibran, to the public service of outstanding leaders like Health and Human Services Secretary Donna Shalala, and so many like her – and to honor Dr. Alice B. Cury Farkouh; and

*W*hereas, on behalf of all Brooklynites, I salute Dr. Farkouh, dedicated educator, active member of St. Mary's Church in Bay Ridge, and proud daughter of Brooklyn by way of Kentucky, whose grandparents hailed from Lebanon and Syria, currently Adjunct Assistant Professor at the College of Staten Island, CUNY, and former principal of Fort Hamilton High School, her alma mater, where initiatives she spearheaded included programs in sports, music, the performing arts, and languages, thereby broadly expanding opportunities for the students under her watch, I commend her for a lifetime of service to the children of Brooklyn, our leaders of tomorrow, and I thank her for contributions that make Brooklyn and New York City a better place to live, work, and raise a family;

*N*ow, therefore, I, Marty Markowitz, President of the Borough of Brooklyn, do hereby confer this citation on

Dr. Alice B. Cury Farkouh

*I*n witness whereof, I have hereunto set my hand and caused the seal of the Borough of Brooklyn to be affixed this 21st day of March, 2006.

President of the Borough of Brooklyn

On March 21, 2006, I was honored with this citation from the Borough President of Brooklyn during the Lebanese Heritage Reception.

A family tree grew in Brooklyn. Its roots intertwined among religions, customs, and languages which stretched back to the mountains of Lebanon, then gently moved along the road to Damascus, swam across the waters of the Atlantic Ocean, where they gripped the shores of America.

A Lebanese-Syrian American Educator fulfills a passion for teaching and learning, and inspires her listeners with her story:

Never Say You Can't...Never Say You Can't...

country like to keep up with their old high school news, reading about reunions, the current principal's letter, and special events.

I didn't actually tell you the truth when I said I had begun the end of my career. Are you kidding? I am just getting started! I am now the principal of a lovely parochial school in Brooklyn Heights, A. Fantis Parochial School of Sts. Constantine and Helen Greek Orthodox Cathedral. The school is located around the corner from the Sts. Constantine and Helen Cathedral on Schermerhorn Street. In just over four years since my arrival, key members of the Church, the School Committee, and I have been able to almost triple the school population. This is just the beginning! The irony of my new position is that the school is located at 195 State Street, only several blocks away from my Mom's old home on State Street; and near my Dad's old home on Third Street. It seems that I have been blessed to continue my education, and continue my passion to help provide an outstanding education for our youth. To be a principal of a Greek Orthodox parochial school, which is the religion of my parents, as well as my ancestors, is quite ironic. Or is it ironic? Has it been a sign from God and the angel who is always watching me from above? Is it possible that my mother and father are above watching over their daughter? What do you think?

On the 21st day of May in the year of Our Lord 2010, the Archbishop Demetrios of America honored me at Sts. Constantine and Helen Cathedral and presented me with *The Archdiocesan Medal of St. Paul*. Father John K. Lardas, our priest, and Hercules Argyriou, the President of Sts. Constantine and Helen Cathedral, informed me that this gift bestowed upon me is the highest honor a layperson can receive from the Greek Orthodox Church of America for recognition of outstanding services and commitment to our Church in America.

I feel very humbled to have received this medal and will always wear it with pride and with dedication to my faith and to my passion, educating young people and inspiring them, as well as others, under my tutelage.

A passion for education and educational leadership brought me back to a school of my own faith where I am today. It's the beginning of the end of a long journey in my field of education. *(October, 2009)*

Receiving the St. Paul Citation on May 21, 2010 at Sts. Constantine and Helen Cathedral: (Center, top row) His Eminence, the Archbishop Demetrios of America. (Bottom row, L to R) I am receiving the citation from our priest, Father John K. Lardas, with the president of the school's Board of Trustees, Hercules Argyriou, standing beside him.
(Photo courtesy Evie Delgado 2010)

What was so meaningful to me on that day was being honored by His Eminence Archbishop Demetrios; being applauded by the Church Community of Sts. Constantine and Helen Cathedral; and having all my students and the faculty of A. Fantis Parochial School present to watch the ceremony after Divine Liturgy. I wonder if one student or teacher present might wish, "One day could this happen to me?" I don't think so, I know so!

My mother and father had to be looking down from Heaven on that day and smiling. Yes, my parents gave me the courage to try, the love to care, and the desire to succeed, as I wrote in my book dedication. My loving husband, Charlie, is always at my side also to support and care about my passion for education, love for our Church, and love for our family.

Our priest, Father John K. Lardas, and I in church. I am proudly wearing my St. Paul Medal. Father John, the community, and I have worked so hard together to build the A. Fantis Parochial School of Sts. Constantine and Helen Cathedral since I first arrived in March of 2006.

"Today's dreams are tomorrow's possibilities."

I have been blessed to be a Lebanese-Syrian American who has searched for the history of her family. I hope that my children, and their children, and many generations to come, will always remember their history, their heritage, and their roots. They have to be proud of the fact that we are part of America's dream to live in a country such as ours, and to serve our country holding our heads high. Yes, Lebanese-Syrian Americans are indeed an ethnic group that can truly say we have contributed in a positive way to our country's history.

Stand tall and remember Never Say You Can't....Never Say You Can't....

(Opposite page) This is one of my favorite pictures of a very familiar sight—sunset on the Verrazano-Narrows Bridge. This double-decked suspension bridge links the boroughs of Staten Island and Brooklyn, and from the time it opened in 1964, it has also been my link to my work, my church, and my family and friends.

(Opposite page) Photo courtesy Michael A. D'Ambrosio FHHS Promotional Brochure 1990-91

When I look at this beautiful sunset on the
Verrazano-Narrows Bridge, it reminds me never to say you
can't reach for the stars. We are here to realize that God has
given us the tools to live in this Universe. Share with others,
and pass on the belief that nothing is impossible if you know that

"...the sunset at the end of the day is a reminder of the
sunrise at the beginning of the next day."